Guten Appetit!

Ute Buehler

© 2015 by Ute Buehler, except where especially referred to otherwise.

All rights reserved. No part of this book may be used or reproduced in any manner whatsoever without written permission except in the case of brief quotations embodied in critical articles and reviews.

For information, write to the publisher, studio 214 publishing,
501 Main Street North Suite 214, Stillwater, Minnesota 55082, U.S.A.
www.studio214publishing.com

Second, revised edition
Design, photos and text © Ute Buehler, except where mentioned otherwise.
ISBN 978-0-977-0749-0-7 Paperback, published 2015
(honored with a Benjamin Franklin Silver Award)
ISBN 978-0-977-0749-9-0 eBook, published 2016

Library of Congress Copyright Office Registration Number TXu 1-939-888, January 22, 2015
Guten Appetit! A Delicious Journey through another Germany

Manufactured in the United States of America

First Edition
ISBN 978-0-977-0749-0-0, published 2006
Copyright © Ute Buehler 2006 All rights reserved
Library of Congress Registration TX6-362-653—2006 Buehler, Ute

Guten Appetit!
With Ute Buehler through Northern Germany's Kitchens—A Delicious Journey
ISBN 0-9770749-0-0

First Printing February 2006, Design, photos and text © Ute Buehler
"Ute B" is a trademark of Ute Buehler

For Chuck, who helped me re-discover my love for
Germany's traditional kitchen

Overview

A Little History   2

    Germany   2
    Prussia   3
    Bohemia   3
    The "Hanse," the Hanseatic League   4
    Europe and the European Union   5
    The Venues of this Book   6
    Converting European to American Measurements   7
    A Little Guide to Pronunciation   8

Venues and Menus   10

A Guide to German Food and Beverages   97

    Basic ingredients in German cooking   97
    Soups and sauces   97
    About American versus German ingredients   97
    A little guide to commonly used herbs and spices   98
    About Beers and Wines   98
    The Beers   98
    The Wines   100
    The Grapes   100
    Mushrooms in Europe   101
    Dieting?   101

Index   103

References   113

Thank You   115

A Little History

Germany

Area: 356,959 square kilometers (about 63% of the size of Minnesota.) Population: 81 million, 20% of which are of non-German nationality.) Population density per sq.kilometer: 227 (in comparison: The U.S.A. average population density per square kilometer is 29, Minnesota 67, Florida 364 and Alaska 1.3.)

Germany today consists of 17 States, 3 of which are so-called City States (Stadtstaaten: Berlin, Hamburg and Bremen)

History: this can only be a very short excursion into German history:. Germany always rivaled countries like France, Italy, Austria and Spain. Endless wars in Central Europe bear witness to this constant struggle for power in the area. The first German Empire was a Federation of German princedoms and kingdoms (between 100 and 290 of them) under an elected Emperor and ended in 1801.

Later on the Second German Empire (1871) was founded by Otto von Bismarck, chancellor of Emperor Wilhelm I. It ended after WWI.

The darkest time in Germany's modern history is the Third Reich under Adolf Hitler. Millions of innocent lives (6 million Jewish people from all over Europe, gays, gypsies, Christian priests and pastors, intellectuals and members of the political opposition) perished in prisons and concentration camps.

After WWII, Germany was divided, first into four sectors (with the Americans in the South,) then into West- and East (Communist) Germany.

With the help of Germany's former enemies, the Allies and especially the U.S.A., the country recovered. The post-war generation of Germany still remembers the Marshal Plan, implemented under President Truman and Herbert Hoover. The Berlin Airlift—Berlin's people called these planes "Raisin Bombers." In 1989, Germany was reunited and now is part of the European Union and the Euro area.

Today's Germany is a parliamentary republic. The "Bundestag" (the parliament, like our House of Representatives) and a "Bundesrat" (the assembly of the states' governors acting somewhat like our Senate in the U.S) govern the country. Germany is represented by the Bundespraesident (president,) who signs laws but doesn't have individual political power. The political power is held by the "Bundeskanzler" the Chancellor as head of the government. The chancellor is elected by the parliament and usually the head of the biggest of the factions of Parliament. Presently, four parties make up Germany's Parliament, directly elected by the people: CDU/CSU as the Conservatives, SPD (Social Democrats mid left,) "Die Linke" (far left liberal) and Green Party liberal with green agenda.

Topographically Germany has the Alps in the South (Bavaria, well known to most Americans as the sites of beautiful Schloss Hohenschwangau, Octoberfest and Hofbrauhaus in Munich,) North Sea and Baltic Sea in the North, and is divided by its two major rivers, the Rhine in the West and the Elbe in the East.

And the country does not lack a "Mason-Dixon-Line," too. It is called the "Weisswurst Äquator" (the veal sausage equator,) along the Main river, which divides Germany South of Frankfurt into a Northern and Southern part.

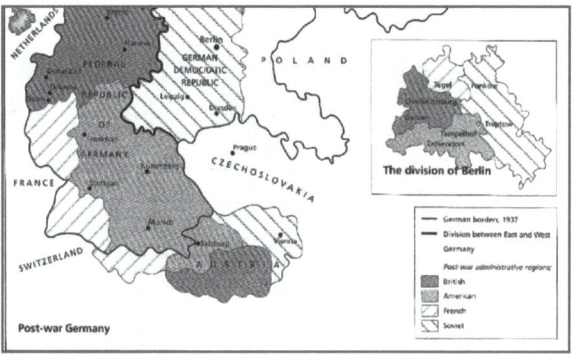

Just to give an idea of the changes that occurred after WWII, here's a map of post-WWII Germany 1945. After WWII 15 million displaced Germans from the former German areas migrated West into the Bundesrepublik Deutschland

I have frequently been asked questions about Prussia and Bohemia, countries where quite a few of Americans' ancestors came from. Here's a short report about these old countries.

Prussia

Prussia's history, you could say, started in the 15th century in the German province of Brandenburg. The House of Hohenzollern took power and eventually expanded its power base into East Prussia and the areas around the Baltic Sea until it became one of the most prominent dynasties in Europe.

With King Frederic II, the Great, around 1740, Prussia was a cultural and political center of all Europe. After the Napoleon Wars Prussia acquired the Rhinelands and thus included about two thirds of the territory and three fourths of the po;ulation of all Germany. The second German Empire under "Kaiser Wilhelm" and Bismarck was founded after Prussia overran France in 1871 and ended after WWI in 1918. However, Berlin continued to be the German capital through the times of the Roaring Twenties, the Third Reich and, after the reunification of the two Germanys, today is German capital again.

Prussia, however, was divided after WWII between Germany, Poland and Russia. Today, the area around old Königsberg is called Kaliningrad and is Russian. The rest of the area belongs to Poland.

German friends of ours keep telling us that we have to go and visit those old places as they are still as beautiful as our forefathers experienced them on their travels. My dad used to tell me stories about the area around the bay of Gdansk, Poland (previously Danzig,) up to Kaliningrad, Russia and its famous natural beauty.

Bohemia

Bohemia, today's Czech Republic, was an independent kingdom since the middle ages. After the Lutheran Reformation in the 16th century Bohemia became protestant. And the Bohemian people being independent and proud, they resisted the attempt of their Austrian King in 1608 to become catholic, thus the Thirty Year (religious) War started right here, in Bohemia. The old Bohemia with Prague as its capital was one of the most powerful political and cultural centers of medieval Europe from the 10th century to the Napoleon times in the beginning of the 19th century. In 1867 Bohemia became part of Austria as a Dual Monarchy. After World War I the Czechoslovac Republic was formed and overrun by the Nazis in 1939, when it became part of the Third Reich.

1945 brought Communism to a combined Czechoslovakia (Bohemia, Slovakia and Moravia) which lasted until 1989. Czechoslovakia separated into two countries, the Czech Republik and Slovakia. Both countries are members of the European Union.

↕ Bohemia 1803
Czech Repuiblik today

The "Hanse," the Hanseatic League

This powerful Europe-wide alliance of cities with trading stations ranging from London to Lisbon, from Bergen to Tallin, from Antwerp to Rostock, could (with a little imagination) be compared to the early beginnings of the European Union, the European Free Trade Association (EFTA.) Powerful through the 14th to 17th centuries, this confederation of merchant guilds and their market towns dominated the trade along the coastline of Northern Europe and the rivers and trade routes leading to them.

Interestingly enough, the Hanseatic cities had their own legal system and their own armies for mutual protection, although the cities themselves were not necessarily autonomous. Still today there are a few cities in Germany carrying the name "Hanse," two of them autonomous, Hansestadt Hamburg and Hansestadt Bremen, both with their own city-state status, their own parliament, their own, independent government.

The Hanseatic League also developed their own architectural style, with its typical brick design, still today found in many cities like Neuss, Stralsund, Rostock, Wismar and Hamburg.

Today, the memory of the "Hanse" is celebrated each year with the "Hansetage" (the Hanseatic Days) in a different one of the former cities of the association. The "Hansetage" of Neuss, sister city of Düsseldorf, were always a huge attraction throughout the region with markets and performances and presentations of costumed artists and tradesmen in the streets, with food and drinks—one event I miss a little bit.

Europe and the European Union

2015 shows a much different image of Europe and the European Union than 2006, when the first Edition of this book was published.

Below left: a map of the political structure of Europe

Below right: a map of the European Union in 2015

Image right: a topographical map of Europe

Sources: Europeean Union, Google maps, www.worldatlasbook.com

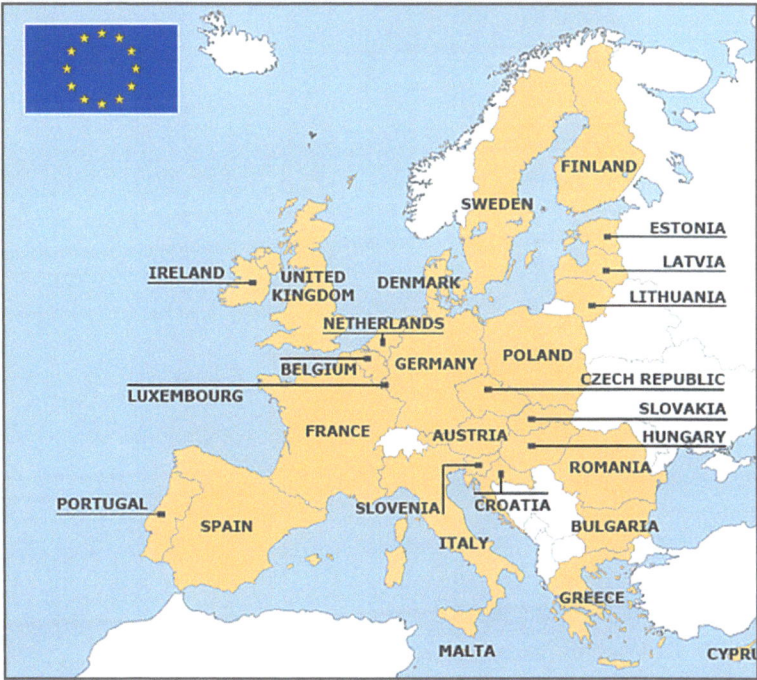

The Venues of this Book

Converting European to American Measurements

Inch =	centimeter
0.05	0.15
0.10	0.25
0.25	0.64
0.30	0.76
0.50	1.27
0.75	1.91
1.00	2.54
2.00	5.08
3.00	7.62
4.00	10.16
5.00	12.70
6.00	15.24
9.00	22.86
12.00	30.48

1 inch = 2.54 cm
12 inches = 1 foot
1 foot = 30 cm = 0.3 meter

100 cm = 1 meter
1,000 meter = 1 kilometer

Fl Oz =	cups =	Tbsp =	tsp =	Litres =	Millilitres
			5 tsp		25 ml
1 oz		1 Tbsp	6 tsp		30 ml
2 oz	1/4 cup	4 Tbsp	12 tsp		60 ml
2.4 oz	1/3 cup	5 Tbsp + 1 tsp	16 tsp		80 ml
4 oz	1/2 cup	8 Tbsp			120 ml
4.1 oz	1/2 cup + 1 tsp	8 Tbsp + 1 tsp		1/8 l	125 ml
4.8 oz	2/3 cup	10 Tbsp + 2 tsp			160 ml
5.3 oz	2/3 cup + 1 Tbsp	11 Tbsp + 2 tsp			150 ml
6 oz	3/4 cup	12 Tbsp			180 ml
6.4 oz	1/2 + 1/3 cup	13 Tbsp + 1 tsp			185 ml
8 oz	1 cup	16 Tbsp			240 ml
8.3 oz	1 cup + 1 tsp	16 Tbsp + 1 tsp		1/4 l	250 ml
	1 cup + 1 Tbsp				275 ml
10 oz	1 1/4 cup				300 ml
10.4 oz	1 1/3 cup				320 ml
	1 1/2 cup - 2 tsp				350 ml
12 oz	1 1/2 cup				360 ml
16.6 oz	2 cups + 2 tsp			1/2 l	500 ml
32 oz	4 cups = 1 quart			0.96 l	960 ml
128 oz	4 quarts = 1 gallon			0.384 l	3840 ml

Celsius =	Fahrenheit
275	525
250	480
230	450
225	435
220	425
200	390
190	375
180	355
175	345
170	335
150	300

Conversion Rule
Celsius = (Fahrenheit - 32) * 5/9
Fahrenheit = (Celsius * 9/5) + 32

Grams =	Ounces	Ounces =	Grams =	Kilograms
1.00	0.04	0.88	25.00	
5.00	0.18	1.00	28.35	
10.00	0.35	3.50	100.00	
15.00	0.53	3.88	125.00	1/8 kg
20.00	0.71	5.25	150.00	
25.00	0.88	6.20	175.00	
50.00	1.77	7.10	200.00	
75.00	2.65	8.00	225.00	
100.00	3.53	8.50	250.00	1/4 kg

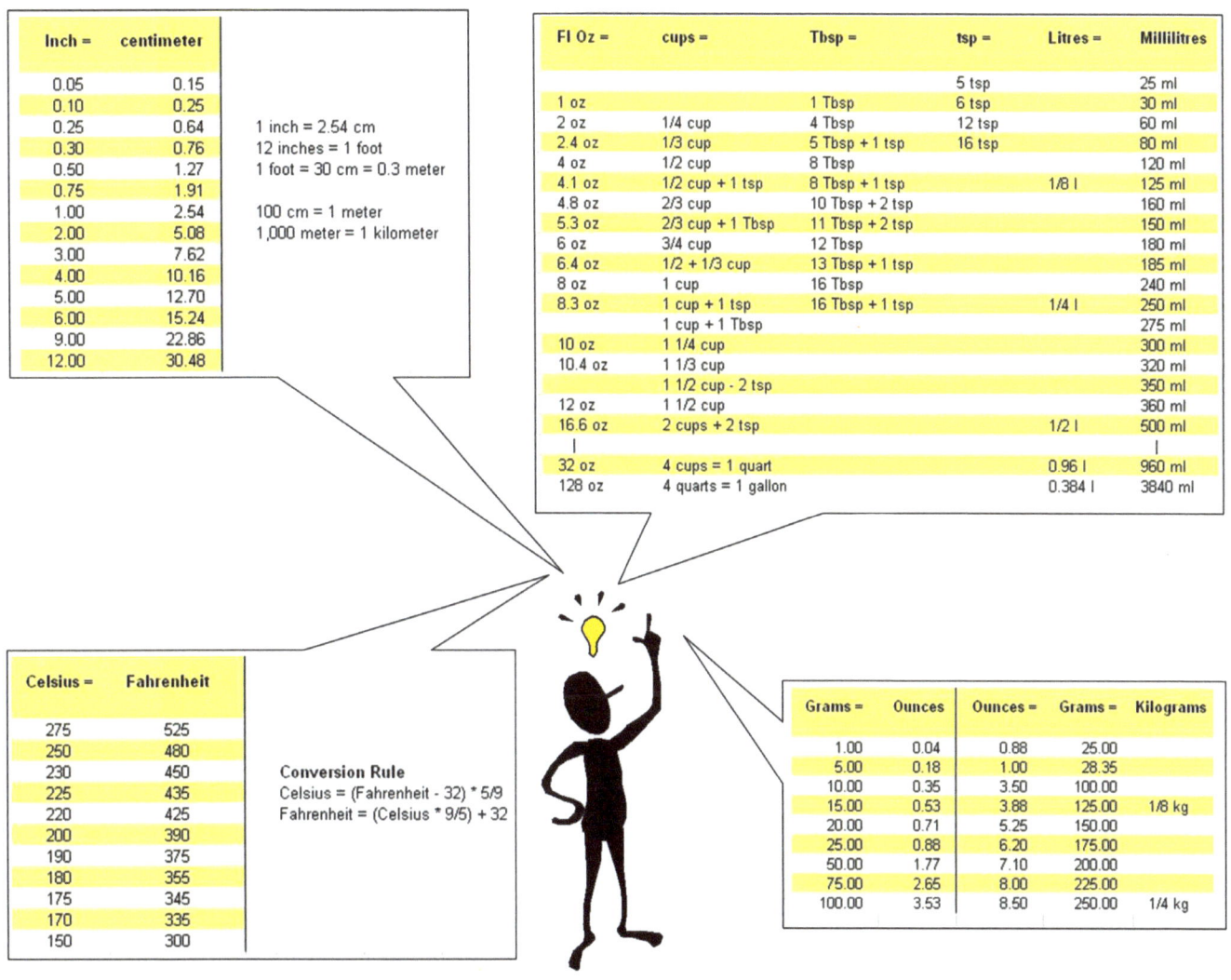

Note: Metric measurements in parentheses in this book are added for the convenience of my readers in countries outside the U.S.

A Little Guide to Pronunciation

Ahr (the river) — AHR
Biedermeier — BEE-dar-my-ar
Bigosh — BEE-gosh
Cevapcici — cha-VAP-tshe-tshe
Cochem — CO-ham (like the Spanish Jalapeno sound)
Düsseldorf — DU-sal-dorf
Eifel — I-fel
Erbsensuppe – ARB-san-zou-pe
Frankfurt - FRAHNK-fourt
Gewürztraminer – ge-WURTS-traa-mee-nar
Glühwein – GLU-vine
Grüner Veltliner – GRU-nar felt-LEE-nar
Karneval – CAHR-na-val
Kirschmichel – KERSH-me-hal
Königsberger Klopse – KO-negs-bar-gar kl-OP-sa
Langenberg – LAHN-gan-barg
Mardi Gras – MAAR-de graa
Matjes – MAHT-yas
Mecklenburg – MAK-lan-bourg
Mosel River – MOU-sal
Moussaka – MOOS-saa-kaa
Osnabrück os-nah-BRUK
Reibekuchen – RI-ba-kou-han
Riesling – REES-ling
Rote Grütze ROU-ta gr-UT-se
Rumtopf – ROOM-topf
Sauerbraten – SOW-ar-brah-tan
Sauvignon Blanc – SAU-ve-gnon BLAHN
Semmelknödel – SAM-mal-kno-dal
Spätburgunder – SHPAT-bour-goun-dar
Speckpfannekuchen – SHPAK-pfahn-na-kou-hen
Tafelspitz –TAH-fal-shpets
Thüringer Klösse – TU-ren-gar KLO-sa
Tsatsiki – tsah-TSE-ke
Xanten – KSAHN-tan

A Few Rules of Pronounciation:

a	The German a is pronounced like the a in ARMY
ä	To make it simple, just pronounce it like the a in "apple"
e	Like the American A
ei	Like the American I
i	Like the American E
ie	Like the American EE
j	Always pronounced like the American Y
ö	Simply put, pronounce it like the o in "word"
s	Pronounce the German s before a vowel like z, before a consonant like sh
ü	The Umlaut of U is pronounced as if you want to whistle with an almost closed mouth
v	v is generally pronounced like the American f, but not always. Sometimes it is pronouced like an American v like in "vase," words deriving from a different language (yes, there are exception in the German language as well)
x	The German X is pronounced as Ks
z	Pronounced like a TS

The Menus of the Month

These menus reflect a collection of recipes, gathered from family and friends, carefully composed and paired with beverages.

The "Extras," the special dishes of the month, are specialties of the individual regions. They are mostly tied to the season or time of the year in this book, trying to give a feeling for the cultural and social background of the region.

Although today's Germans do not follow the traditionally (for formal events) strict sequence of

Appetizer

Soup

Salad

Entrée

Side salad

Side dishes

Dessert

All menus are paired with the appropriate beverages, it was fun to compose these menus for you, the reader's, selection.

Enjoy!

Venues and Menus

January in Xanten

Soup: Clear tomato soup   16
Entrée: Rouladen (stuffed beef) with a stew of carrots and potatoes "Durcheinander"   16
Side dish: Carrot and potato dish (Durcheinander)   17
Side salad: Lambs' lettuce (Feldsalat) with mustard dressing and bacon crumbles   17
Dessert: Rote Grütze with vanilla ice cream or yogurt cream   17
Special dish of the month: New Year's Herring Salad   18

February in Düsseldorf

Appetizer: Leek Quiche   22
Soup: Mock turtle soup (my family version)   22
Entrée: Sauerbraten with red cabbage, Thuringian dumplings and applesauce with cranberries   22
Beverage: Red wine like Cabernet Sauvignon, Red Zinfandel, or Pinot Noir   23
Side dish: Red cabbage and Thuringian dumplings   23
Dessert: Brigitte's Yogurt cake and alternatively a German cheesecake   24
Special dish of the month: Erbsensuppe (split pea soup)   25

March in Berlin

Appetizer: Fennel salad with orange-caper dressing   30
Soup: Clear beef bouillon with pancake strips   30
Entrée: Chicken ragout à la Berlin with rice   31
Beverage: Riesling white wine   32
Side Salad: Iceberg lettuce with almond lemon dressing   32
Dessert: Sweet rice in red wine with whipped cream (Reisflammeri)   32
Special dish of the month: Meerrettichlende (or Tafelspitz,) beef loin with horseradish and chives cream   32

April in the Bergische Land

Appetizer: Butter Beans salad   38
Soup: Creamed potato soup with leek julienne   38
Entrée: Ragout from calf tongue with a side dish of cauliflower baked in puff pastry   38
Beverage: White wine like Chardonnay or Pinot Grigio   39
Side salad: Romaine lettuce with creamy mustard dressing and walnuts   39
Dessert: Cold sweet strawberry soup (Erdbeerkaltschale)   39
Special dish of the month: Haddock fillets in creamy mustard sauce baked with vegetable julienne   40

May in Osnabrück

Appetizer: Marinated Salmon à la Ingeborg   44
Soup: Clear white asparagus soup with asparagus pieces   44
Entrée: White asparagus with melted golden butter, new potatoes, and sliced cooked ham   44
Beverage: White Burgundy   45
Side Salad: Carrot salad with sweet and sour dressing   45
Dessert: Rhubarb-vanilla cream   45
Special dish of the month: Matjes (young herring fillets) with new potatoes in a creamy sauce   46

June in Köln (Cologne)

Appetizer: Celery root (celeriac,) fried, in a lemon dressing with walnuts or pumpkin seeds   52
Soup: Goulash soup   52
Entrée: Kohlrouladen (pigs in a blanket) with potatoes, carrots, and gravy   52
Beverage: Kölsch beer or a dry white wine like Pinot Grigio or Orvieto   53
Side salad: Mushroom salad with garlic lemon vinaigrette   53
Ingredients (serves 4):   53
Dessert: Chocolate cake à la Elisabeth   53
Special dish of the month: Himmel und Erde (Heaven and Earth) with chicken liver or fried black pudding   54

July in Frankfurt am Main

Appetizer: Mixed bell pepper salad with Italian dressing   58
Soup: Vegetable soup with egg dumplings   58
Entrée: Mushroom Schnitzel with green beans in creamy mushroom sauce   59
Beverage: Red Zinfandel or Roter Spätburgunder (Red Burgundy) from Germany   60
Side salads: Tomato salad with red onion vinaigrette or Spinach salad with mustard dressing   60
Dessert: Kirschmichel (Cherry Crumble)   60
Special dish of the month: Sauerkraut Quiche   61

August on the Mosel River

Appetizer: Belgian endive with mandarin oranges in sour cream dressing   66
Soup: Chicken bouillon with semolina dumplings   66
Entrée: Sole with carrot cream on risotto and kohlrabi   67
Beverage: Riesling or light beer   67
Side salad: Cucumber salad with dill dressing   67
Dessert: Peach Mousse   67
Special dish of the month: Mini meatloaves in mushroom sauce   68

September in the Ahr Valley

Appetizer: Zwiebelkuchen (onion pie)   72
Soup: Mushroom cream soup   72
Entrée: Pheasant or Cornish game hen with wine sauerkraut and Portobello mashed potatoes   72
Beverage: Red Zinfandel or Shiraz   73
Side salad: Mixed greens with cream of chives   73
Dessert: Pears sautéed in red Burgundy wine   74
Alternative dessert: Chocolate mousse   74
Special dish of the month: Rabbit in white wine sauce, paired with Karin's potato gratin   74

October in the Eifel Mountains

Appetizer: Pasta salad with white crab meat   80
Soup: Pumpkin soup with julienne of leek and carrot   80
Entrée: Mushroom ragout with Pfannekuchen (German pancakes)   80
Side salad: Romaine lettuce with lemon tarragon dressing   81
Beverage: Red wine like Merlot or Pilsner beer   81
Dessert: Dorothea's Pflaumenkuchen (Plumcake)   81
Special dish of the month: Pork tenderloin in beer sauce with apples and cranberries, dried fruit compote or creamed savoy cabbage   82

November on the Baltic Sea

Appetizer: Beets and Oranges with an orange and horseradish cream dressing   86
Soup: Herbed soup   86
Entrée: Mecklenburg fish ragout   86
Beverage: Gewürztraminer or Sauvignon Blanc   87
Side salad: Biedermeier potato salad   87
Dessert: Bread pudding or wine cream   87
Special dish of the month: Gundula's beef loin with apples, plums, and potatoes   88

December at the Christmas Markets

Appetizer: Bean salad and shrimp with a lime vinaigrette   92
Soup: Creamed Tomato soup with sherry wine   92
Entrée: Loin of deer with Brussels sprouts and Semmelknödel (bread dumplings)   92
Side salad: Arugula salad with vinaigrette, cranberries and walnuts   93
Beverage: Pinot Noir or a Red Burgundy   93
Dessert: Baked apples in vanilla sauce   93
A little Christmas treat: Spekulatius cookies   94
Special dish: Reibekuchen (potato pancakes) and Glühwein   95
Another Special: Hasenpfeffer (sweet and sour hare,) my family's Christmas dinner   96

January in Xanten

Xanten, Niederrhein, close to the Netherlands' Border

January in Xanten

The Niederrhein region, on the western side of the Rhine River, begins just north of Düsseldorf in the Duisburg area and ends at the German-Dutch border.

The history of Xanten, a city located close to the Dutch border, goes way back to Roman times when the city was one of the most important fortresses along the Germanic-Roman border. From here the Roman general Varus took his army to defeat the Germanic tribes under Arminius, Prince of the Cherusci (also known as Hermann der Cherusker) — and Varus was defeated by the Germans.

The Roman army built barracks and a fortress in Xanten in 15 B.C., and excavations have found a thriving Roman city. The old Roman fortress is now a museum showing how Romans lived about 2,000 years ago. And Xanten has taken advantage of the wonderfully preserved ruins to rebuild the ancient Roman city, its baths, living quarters and, of course, its arena, the amphitheater. These very well-restored buildings, baths, gymnasiums, kitchens, and houses offer an exciting Sunday excursion for families and a must-have field trip for schools in the area.

Also, the town itself is full of quaint old buildings from the early middle ages, including a cathedral built in the 13th century. Old Dutch windmills were built in the 17th century, to mill flour until the beginning of the 20th century, so they are also today's tourist attractions throughout the area. Step stones like the lion pictured are found next to the entries of some of the old houses. The Klever Tor (gate to the road to the City of Kleve,) built in 1393, serves today as a museum.

If you, like I am, are an opera fan and like to watch real-life opera open air performances, this is the place to go (unless you'd like to travel to Verona, Italy.) I attended a performance of George Bizet's opera "Carmen," and it was spectacular, starting at dusk on a warm June night and ending around midnight. Everybody had brought along a picnic dinner, a blanket to sit on. And as you never know what the weather will be like – an umbrella.

Pictures from top right clockwise: Klever Tor, Windmill, City Wall, typical street in Xanten, Lion stepstone, Kopfweide (willow,) window of an antique shop, area map

The Niederrhein region has many other very old and quaint cities in addition to Xanten. Tourism is an ever-growing local "industry," in addition to science and the arts. This area is flat like the Great Plains in the mid-western United States. I love the typical vistas, a flat land with small creeks lined by Kopfweiden (willow trees,) and long rows of poplar trees.

The branches of these willow trees are cut down to the stump, and branches and twigs are the base product for the area's willow weaving industry. We used to take long bike rides around the lakes of this area, also called the "Kannenbäcker Land" (the land of the pottery bakers.) The Niederrhein area produces pottery, which is well known all over the country. In December, you find their products – wonderfully woven baskets, ceramic candle holders and vases, bowls, and plates, even flutes – in Christmas markets all over the area.

About the Menu

Soups are an important part of any traditional German meal. In my family, most Sunday meals started with a cup of soup. The second course would be meat, chicken, or game, with potatoes, pasta or rice, a good share of vegetables and a side salad. A dessert would be the third course.

As soups as a starter are not as common in America, I have added an appetizer as a starter that would go with the menu and could be served instead of the soup.

"Durcheinander" dishes (a kind of stew) were a big part of our meals as a child. Potatoes were mixed with carrots or sauerkraut or cabbage and cooked together with the vegetables so that the juices would mix well. However, I never knew a crockpot until I came to America.

In my childhood, there would be meat only once a week. The other days (fish on Fridays, of course) we would have veggies, noodles and maybe something that is made with ground meat (mostly half-and-half – pork and beef mixed.)

So, here's the Sunday version of one of my favorites, Rouladen, stuffed beef. I have found this dish all over Germany and Europe in as many local variations as there are locations.

January in Xanten

Appetizer:
Cucumber and tomato salad with onions and yogurt dressing

Soup:
Clear tomato soup

Entrée:
Rouladen (stuffed beef rolls) with
a stew of carrots and potatoes dish

Side salad:
Lamb's lettuce (or arugula)
in mustard dressing with bacon crumbles

Beverage:
Pilsner or another light beer

Dessert:
Rote Gruetze with vanilla ice cream
or vanilla yogurt cream

Special dish of the month:
New Year's herring salad

Appetizer: Cucumber and tomato salad with onions and yogurt dressing

Ingredients (serves 4):
1 cucumber English style, thinly sliced
1 Tbsp salt
4 medium sized tomatoes, sliced, seeds and white removed
4 Tbsp white onion, finely chopped, (about ½ small onion)
Parsley for garnish

Dressing:
3 tsp plain yogurt
pepper and salt to taste
pinch of sugar

Preparation:
Sprinkle cucumbers with salt and let sit for about 15 minutes. (This helps drain the water from the cucumbers) Drain cucumbers by pressing carefully into a colander. Then arrange cucumbers on the dishes like a wheel. Place tomatoes on top of the cucumbers in the middle also arranged as a wheel so that the outside of the cucumbers can still be seen. Spoon dressing over the middle of the pile so that the tomatoes can still be seen. Place 1 tsp of the chopped white onions in the middle of the dressing. Garnish onions with some parsley.

Note: This would work with American cucumbers as well, but in Germany you use those only to make pickles. Salad cucumbers are the English style cucumbers. You can use canned tomatoes as well, but this is not something a German homemaker would do. However, if you use the diced canned tomatoes, drain carefully before using.

Soup: Clear tomato soup

Ingredients (serves 4):
2 cans diced tomatoes
2 cups (1/2 liter) chicken broth or vegetable broth
1 Tbsp olive oil
1 clove garlic, finely chopped
2 stalks (ribs) of celery, diced
1 small onion, chopped
1 dash balsamic vinegar, or lemon juice
1 Tbsp red wine (optional)
pinch sugar
Italian herbs, or at least ½ tsp thyme
salt and pepper to taste
Fresh basil leaves (best is the top of a basil leaf stem with its crown) for garnish. If you don't have basil, a little sprig of parsley is fine as well.

Preparation:
In a saute pan, heat olive oil to medium heat. Add garlic, onion and celery and stir until onion is transparent. Add diced tomatoes and chicken broth, and bring to a boil. Add vinegar or lemon juice and wine, sugar, salt, freshly ground black pepper, and herbs. Simmer for about 3 minutes, vegetables should still be a little crunchy. Serve in soup cups, and garnish with fresh basil or parsley leaves.

Note: For a formal dinner, this soup would be served between appetizer and entrée. My mom used to top it with a teaspoon of unsweetened whipped cream placed on top of the soup and then place the basil leaves or parsley sprig on top of the whipped cream. This soup looks great and tastes wonderful.

Entrée: Rouladen (stuffed beef) with a stew of carrots and potatoes "Durcheinander"

Ingredients (serves 4):
4 thin (¼") slices beef sirloin, about ¼ lb each
pepper and salt to taste
pinch of sugar
3 Tbsp vegetable oil
8 ounces (1 cup/¼ liter) of mushroom heads, chopped (preferably Portobello,) or 2 cups chopped fresh mushrooms
1 finely chopped small onion
1 Tbsp finely chopped parsley
1 cup (1/4 liter) beef broth or bouillon
3 Tbsp heavy cream
2 Tbsp red wine

Preparation:
Place the rouladen slices on a cutting board and rub in pepper and salt. Mix onion with mushrooms and parsley. Place mixture in the middle of each roulade and carefully roll up the roulade. Fix with a toothpick so they don't fall apart. Bring oil in the pan to high heat and brown rouladen on all sides (about 10 minutes.) Reduce heat to a simmer, add broth or bouillon, cover pan and simmer for about 50 minutes depending on the size of the rouladen. Take them out of pan and set aside. Add wine, sugar, pepper and salt to pan and bring to a boil, stirring continuously. Remove pan from heat and stir in cream. If you like your sauce a little thicker, add 1 tsp potato starch to the cream before adding it to the sauce. Bring to a boil again, constantly stirring until thick.

Alternative stuffing (my personal favorite): Spread 1 Tbsp yellow mustard on each roulade. Place 1 thin layer of bacon on top, then place 1 small kosher pickle in the middle, and roll them up. Proceed as described above.

For the Rouladen sauce — leaner cooking wanted?:

My mom used to add heavy cream, but I find that a light sour cream is just as good as heavy cream and less fattening.

The traditional German way was to add a pinch of sugar to most dishes, yummy ... but ... there are people who want it slim. For those, I would recommend that they replace the sugar and wine with just a few drops of balsamic vinegar.

Gluten and/or Lactose problems:
To achieve lactose-free sauce: Use 3 Tbsp yogurt mixed with 1 tsp cornstarch to bind it. Substitute this mixture for the heavy cream.

Side dish: Carrot and potato dish (Durcheinander)

Ingredients (serves 4):
8 big carrots, peeled and cut into 1" cubes
8 medium sized potatoes cut into 1" cubes
pinch of sugar
1 Tbsp butter
½ cup (1/8 liter) of water
1 tsp corn starch
pepper and salt
Parsley for decoration, finely chopped

Preparation:
The easiest way to prepare this dish is to steam the vegetables until they are almost tender. Then do the following: in a cooking pan melt 1 Tbsp butter over medium heat, stir in the sugar, add the cooked vegetables and gently stir until all are covered. Mix water with cornstarch and add to vegetables, stir until the all are covered with a nice smooth film. Add salt, pepper and sugar to taste. Serve sprinkled with chopped parsley.

Note: If you don't have a steamer, cook vegetables in as little water as possible, then drain and proceed from there.

Beverage: Pilsner or another light beer

Side salad: Lambs' lettuce (Feldsalat) with mustard dressing and bacon crumbles

Ingredients (serves 4):
4 cups of lambs' lettuce
2 Tbsp crumbled bacon
1 Tbsp mustard or to taste
3 Tbsp walnut oil
2 Tbsp white wine vinegar
Dash lemon juice
1 tsp water
white pepper and salt to taste
2 Tbsp cashew nuts

Optional: Chopped egg white from a hard boiled egg

Preparation
Lambs' lettuce is also known as Mache or field lettuce. Wash lettuce and drain. In a bowl, mix the rest of ingredients together, add lettuce. Toss and garnish with nuts and chopped egg white.

Dessert: Rote Grütze with vanilla ice cream or yogurt cream

Ingredients (serves 4):
1-quart cherries or strawberries, fresh or frozen
1 quart (2 lbs) raspberries, fresh or frozen
1 Tbsp water or red fruit juice as necessary
1 Tbsp sugar
2 Tbsp cornstarch (or more if necessary)
2 Tbsp Cherry or Raspberry Schnapps or other clear Fruit Schnapps. If you don't want to add liquor, use water or juice
1 dash lemon juice
½ tsp vanilla extract or ground vanilla

Preparation:
Clean and prepare fruit, removing stems. If you use frozen fruit, thaw before using. Place about two-thirds of the fruit in a large saucepan. Pour juice into a pan, if needed. Slowly bring to a boil over medium heat, adding vanilla extract, lemon juice, and sugar to taste.

Meanwhile, measure cornstarch into a small bowl and add a little cold water, juice or Schnapps to make a smooth liquid. Remove pan with the hot fruit mixture from the heat and slowly add the cornstarch mixture to the fruit, stirring constantly. Return pan to a low heat and stirring constantly. When it comes to a boil, reduce heat and simmer for about one minute.

While stirring, add the remaining fruit and additional lemon juice, vanilla and sugar to taste. Cool before serving. The consistency should not be as firm as jello or as runny as custard, but just that perfect point in between.

How to serve:
Transfer to a decorative bowl. Serve with a jug of cold milk or half-and-half for pouring on the grütze, which is the traditional German way. However, it also goes very nicely topped with vanilla ice cream or whipped cream.

Note: All fruit should be fresh but if only frozen fruit is available, reduce the amount of water added. I prefer cherries for this dish, but if you can't find fresh, frozen or canned cherries, try ½ lb of dried cherries dissolved in 1 quart of boiling water. Let stand overnight; they should have expanded to their normal size by then. I use very little sugar because Rote Grütze is meant to be quite tart. Rote Gruetze is supposed to be like a fluffy pudding, so I use cornstarch and as little water as possible to achieve this consistency.

Special dish of the month: New Year's Herring Salad

Every family has a different tradition of celebrating the New Year's Eve with dinner. In many parts of Germany, it's fish, carp. (There is this famous story of the couple who bought a living carp home to have it really fresh for dinner. They kept the animal in the bathtub for a few days and then they couldn't get themselves to kill the poor beast.)

So, my dad used to prepare the dinner for New Year's Day. And traditionally we had this very tasty salad because it was so easy to prepare. My mom was supposed to have a day off without cooking and just enjoy the holiday.

I believe that this dish comes from the old East German part of Silesia, because later on, I found it in families that had come as refugees from those old parts of pre-WWII Germany. I also found it in families whose ancestors had come from Poland.

Serve this herring salad with crusty bread and preferably, beer or crisp white wine, like Pinot Grigio.

Ingredients (serves 4):
2 lbs leftover veal or beef cut into ½" cubes
14 halves of herring fillets, cut into ½" cubes
½ cup (100 g) kosher pickled cucumbers, cut into ½" pieces
4 big apples cut into ½" cubes, (tart like Braeburn apples)
1½ cups (300 g) canned beets, drained and cut into ½" cubes
3 Tbsp beet juice
1 Tbsp mayonnaise
1 tsp lemon juice
pepper and salt
parsley for garnish

Preparation:
Mix meat with herring fillets, pickles, apples and beets. Combine beet juice, mayonnaise and lemon juice, adding pepper and salt to taste. Add to meat mixture and toss gently until all ingredients are covered well. Refrigerate for at least 1 hour before serving.

Garnish with parsley, finely chopped, or added as a bouquet. Serve with Schwarzbrot (recipe see "Schwarzbrot" on page 26.)

Note: It is best to cut herring, apples, meat, beets and pickles into same-size pieces.

February in Düsseldorf

Düsseldorf Rhine Promenade

February in Düsseldorf

Düsseldorf and Neuss, its sister city on the other side of the Rhine river, are similar to Minnesota's "Twin Cities" of Minneapolis and St. Paul. Neuss (population 150,000,) an ancient town founded by the Romans in 16 B.C., has been an important member of the trade alliance "Hanse," the old European Hanseatic League, ever since the early Middle Ages.

Düsseldorf (population 600,000) has been a city with all city rights since 1288, and it breathes history. It became the capital of a thriving princedom with Duke Jan Wellem as the legendary prince who brought culture, arts, and pomp and circumstance to the city, creating the beautiful buildings of the Altstadt (the old city,) the Schlossturm (the remaining tower of a destroyed castle on the riverfront,) and other castles around the area. And you can also find traces of the "good old days" between the 13th and 18th centuries everywhere around the old town. In neighborhoods like Gerresheim, Oberkassel, Niederkassel and others, houses are dating back to the early 13th century. One of the city's beloved traditions is the famous Düsseldorf Karneval, a type of Mardi Gras. The Karneval season goes from November 11 to Ash Wednesday, with street celebrations, costumes, and parties. The other grand event is the summer "Kirmes," a huge carnival, comparable to the Munich Oktoberfest.

Today Düsseldorf has a population that includes every ethnic, political and cultural background, the largest Japanese colony in Europe, and a spoken dialect that's quite similar to the Dutch language. Coming into Düsseldorf the first impression is that of a beautiful, modern, and, above all, a "green city." Wide promenades and parks are everywhere, as well as street cafes and restaurants. The busy Old Town is famous as a tourist attraction throughout the whole region and the Netherlands, and the Old Town's "Kneipen," the pubs, are always full of people who just come to eat, drink (mostly beer,) chat, and enjoy. Meeting with friends in a Kneipe is part of the joy of daily life.

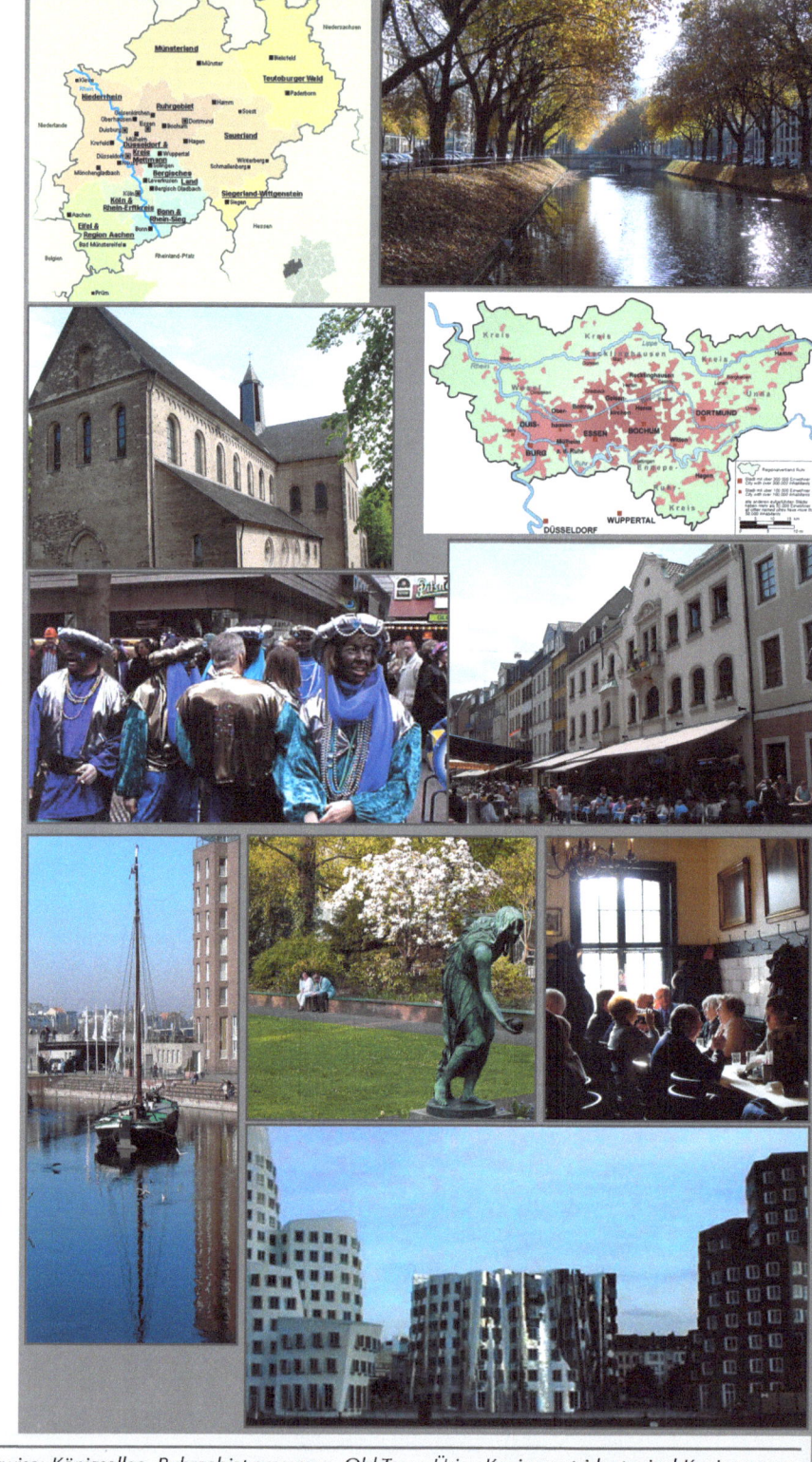

Pictures from top right clockwise: Königsallee, Ruhrgebiet area map, Old Town Ürige Kneipe outside, typical Kneipe scene, Media Harbor Gehry buildings, Old Town Harbor, in the park, Karneval fun, Kaiserswerth Dom, map pf North-Rhine-Westfalia

The "Kö," nickname for Düsseldorf's Königsallee, is a famous shopping boulevard like the Champs Elysée. It has earned the city the nickname "Little Paris" because it has every famous fashion house, glitzy malls, and cafes —all you need to enjoy, and to spend a lot of money. Düsseldorf became a center of the fashion industry after World War II, sharing this fame with cities like Munich and Hamburg. And, as the capital of North-Rhine-Westphalia, it is also nicknamed "the office desk of the Ruhrgebiet," because it has so many corporate headquarters. By the way, over the past 40 years the old "Ruhrgebiet" (the former Ruhr Industrial Area, with its steel and mining productions between Duisburg and Dortmund,) has transformed itself. It is now an area of tourist attractions with theaters, museums, parks, recreational and shopping centers well worth a visit.

During the past decades the media industry has moved into the old Düsseldorf harbor area, and world-famous architects like Frank Gehry have taken special pride in adding their personal touch to the Media Harbor river front. The Frank Gehry buildings are world famous.

About the Menu

Oh yes, Grandma's sauerbraten. It was always a feast and only presented for special occasions like family get-togethers, etc.; not surprising, as its preparation needs to be planned a week ahead of the dinner.

Leek, carrots, and celeriac have an important role in German cooking. You can buy them bundled together in every supermarket. It's called "Suppengemüse" (soup veggies) and contains 2 carrots, 1 piece of leek, 1 quarter of celery root and a sprig of parsley. It is unimaginable to cook soup without these ingredients because they give the soup or broth just the right aroma and then are taken out before serving. You'll read more about them in later recipes, too.

As far as German cheesecake is concerned, it is made with Quark (a by-product of fat-free milk, and an ingredient I have yet to find in American grocery stores. However, I have found it on the Internet, made by a California dairy farm, and sold at the "Deutsche Haus" in several cities. As a substitute, here is an easy variation of a yogurt cake that my friend Brigitte loves to make. It's easy, delicious and light.

And the "Erbsensuppe" (German split pea soup) is a must-have at all carnivals in the Rhineland area, hearty, and good soul food accompanied by Schwarzbrot, the original dark rye bread.

February in Düsseldorf
(Karneval – Mardi Gras – Lent)

Appetizer:
Leek Quiche

Soup:
Mock turtle soup

Entrée:
Grandma's sauerbraten with red cabbage, Thuringian dumplings, and apple sauce

Dessert:
Brigitte's yogurt cake and the alternative German cheesecake

Beverage:
Red wines like Cabernet Sauvignon, Red Zinfandel, or Pinot Noir

Special dish of the month:
"Erbsensuppe" (split pea soup) and Schwarzbrot, the German dark rye bread

Appetizer: Leek Quiche

Ingredients (serves 4):
For the dough:
½ cup plus 1 Tbsp (125g) butter or margarine
1 tsp salt
1 cup plus 1 Tbsp (250g) flour
3 Tbsp cold water
Butter to grease a 9" springform pan
For the filling:
2 lbs (1kg) leek, washed, drained and cut into ¼" squares
1 1/3 cups (300g) smoked bacon, diced
1/3 cup (50g) butter
2 cups (½ l) hot beef broth or bouillon
Salt, pepper and nutmeg to taste
4 eggs
1 cup (1/4 l) half & half
4 Tbsp flour or 2 Tbsp corn starch

Preparation:
Gently blend all ingredients for the dough, form a ball and refrigerate for 30 minutes. Grease a 9" springform pan, and spread dough on the bottom and up the sides. Melt 1/3 cup butter and cook bacon in butter until the fat is melted, and the bacon is crisp. Stir in leeks, and add hot broth and salt, pepper and nutmeg to taste (The egg mixture will be seasoned as well, so be careful.) Cook for 5 to 8 minutes. Drain in a colander, and sprinkle leek and bacon on top of the dough.

Mix eggs with half & half and flour or cornstarch. Season with pepper, salt and nutmeg and pour over the leeks and bacon. Bake for 20 minutes in a preheated oven at 350°F, or until a wooden toothpick comes out clean, and no liquid comes to the top when you press it carefully.

Note: For a quick side dish prepare this in the microwave without the dough. Cover loosely and microwave on high for 2 minutes, then let sit for another 3 minutes before serving. I love this leek quiche as a full meal for supper, with a dry white wine like Pinot Grigio.

How to clean leek: With a sharp knife cut leek stalk lengthwise to the center only, then unfold and wash every part under cold water until free of soil.

Soup: Mock turtle soup (my family version)

Ingredients (serves 4):
1 small onion, finely chopped
1 tsp butter and 2 tsp olive oil
1 lb (1/2 kg) calf tongue or oxtail (preferably oxtail)
1 whole clove
1 pinch thyme
1 bay leaf
3 cups (750 ml) hot water
3 cups chicken stock
Salt and pepper
¼ thin-skinned lemon, chopped (rind and all)
1 Tbsp parsley, finely chopped
4 Tbsp Sherry or Madeira wine

Preparation:
In a 4-quart stock pot brown onion in the butter and oil. Add oxtails or pre-cooked calf tongue and brown slightly. Add the spices and herbs. Pour in the hot water and stock, and bring to a boil. Add all remaining ingredients, except the sherry or Madeira wine. Simmer for 2 hours. Remove the oxtail or tongue, discard the bones, cut the meat into pea sized pieces and return to the soup. Add sherry. To serve, top with chopped parsley and, if you wish, a dab of whipped cream.

Note: Turtle meat was extremely expensive when it was still available before turtles became a protected species. My dad used to make this recipe, as a clear soup, with small pieces of meat and a good sip of Sherry or Madeira wine. There are other recipes like the famous American (meatier and not clear) or the British (Lady Curzon) variations.

Entrée: Sauerbraten with red cabbage, Thuringian dumplings and applesauce with cranberries

Ingredients (serves 4):
Marinade (meat should be in marinade for at least 5 days):
2 cups (500 ml) water
1 cup (250 ml) red wine vinegar
1 tsp salt
3 medium sized onions
1 medium sized carrot
5 cloves
10 Juniper berries
(substitute 2 tsp Gin, if berries are not available)

10 peppercorns
1/2 tsp ground or powdered mustard
2 bay leaves
1 pinch each coriander or cardamom and marjoram
1 tsp rosemary

Meat:
2½ lbs beef for pot roast (e.g. shoulder)
peanut oil or vegetable oil to brown meat

Sauce:
1 cup (250 g) raisins
2 medium sized white onions diced
1 Tbsp molasses
1 tsp apple cider or apple juice
(replace molasses and apple juice with German Apfelkraut, if available)
1/2 cup (125 ml) sour cream
salt and pepper
1/2 cup red wine

Preparation:
Marinating the meat:
Place meat in a Ziplock bag, big enough to hold the meat and the liquid. Mix marinade ingredients and pour over meat, turning several times, so meat is covered on all sides. Place bag in a deep bowl, cover and refrigerate for 5 days, turn the bag twice a day.

Cooking the meat:
Preheat oven to 350 Deg. F. (175 Deg. C.)
Remove meat from marinade and pat dry. Reserve marinade.

In a large Dutch oven brown meat on all sides in very hot oil. Reduce heat. Add raisins and diced onions and simmer with the meat for 15 minutes. Slowly add marinade and red wine, plus a shot of brandy if desired.

Cover dutch oven and place in preheated oven for about 3 hours, or more, until meat is tender. Remove meat and let rest in a warm place.

Blend sauce in a blender. Return sauce to Dutch oven and let cook for another 10 minutes, adding molasses, apple juice, salt, and pepper.

Add sliced green onions, if wanted, and sour cream to taste.

Serve with red cabbage and potato dumplings or peeled, boiled potatoes. If red cabbage is not to your taste, a side dish of brokkoli or carrots will be as good. Traditionally this dish is served with a side of applesauce and cranberries.

Note: Green onions are used today but are not one of the original ingredients.

Beverage: Red wine like Cabernet Sauvignon, Red Zinfandel, or Pinot Noir

Side dish: Red cabbage and Thuringian dumplings

Red cabbage

Ingredients (serves 4):
1 head red cabbage cut into bite-size pieces
2 Tbsp bacon drippings, lard or vegetable oil
4 Tbsp balsamic vinegar
3 apples, peeled and diced
Water or apple juice, if needed
6 cloves
½ onion chopped
salt, sugar, cinnamon (1 pinch each)

Preparation:
Heat drippings, lard or oil, and saute cabbage. Add vinegar and stir until completely dry. Add apples, onion and cloves. Add water, salt and cinnamon, and maybe some powdered cloves, to taste. Simmer until it's as soft as you like it.

Variation: Add cranberry jelly before serving and simmer for 2 more minutes.

Thuringian Dumplings

Ingredients (serves 4):
4 potatoes
milk, salt
3 rolls or toast, rind cut off, diced, or croutons
Butter for toast

Preparation:
Peel potatoes. Grate 3 potatoes into a large pot of cold water. Drain carefully. Refill the pot with cold water, and repeat this procedure until water is clear. Cook or steam the fourth potato, mash it very finely and mix with milk.

Press grated raw potatoes through a fine mesh into a deep bowl. Use a fork to loosen, add salt and hot mashed potatoes. Mix well and form dumplings. If the dumpling mixture is too thin, add 1 tsp potato starch. Dice rolls and roast in butter until golden brown (or use croutons.) Press one or two croutons into the middle of each dumpling. Place dumplings in simmering water and simmer for 15-20 minutes. Don't let the water boil.

Instead of side salad: Applesauce with cranberries

Ingredients (serves 4):
8 apples like Braeburn, cored, peeled and quartered
4 cloves
½ tsp cinnamon
½ tsp vanilla extract
1 Tbsp water
Sugar to taste
Lemon juice to taste (optional,) only if apples are too sweet
4 Tbsp of whole cranberries, from can, for decoration

Preparation
Place apples in a saucepan, add spices and water (lemon juice just not yet) and bring to a boil. Reduce heat to minimum and simmer until apples are tender and can be mashed with a fork.

Remove from heat, remove cloves and add lemon juice if necessary. Serve on individual dishes topped with one Tbsp of cranberries each.

Note: The apple sauce is served with the meal as a side dish. The apple used would be a "Boskop" apple. In the US I prefer a Braeburn; the best choice is a tart, juicy apple. In Germany, Preiselbeeren are the local kind of cranberries. Usually, we would add a spoonful of cranberry jelly or compote in the middle for decoration.

Dessert: Brigitte's Yogurt cake and alternatively a German cheesecake

Ingredients:
2 eggs or 1 egg plus 1 egg white, beaten
1 cup plain yogurt
3 cups flour
2 cups powdered sugar
½ Tbsp baking powder
1 Tbsp vanilla extract + 1 Tbsp sugar
3 Tbsp vegetable oil
½ cup raisins, soaked in warm water for 30 minutes (50g)
¼ cup Rum or Rum extract
1 Tbsp butter to grease the spring form pan

Preparation:
Preheat oven to 350°F (180°C)

Mix all ingredients in the order given above. Blend carefully. Pour mixture into a greased 9" spring form pan and bake 45 minutes at 350°F. Turn off the heat, open oven a crack, and let cool in oven, so the cake doesn't collapse.

Note: If you have a cholesterol problem, use only the beaten egg white of the second egg and discard the egg yolk.

An alternative: Monika's German Cheese Cake with raisins

Preheat oven to 350°F (180°C)

Here's one of the numerous traditional German "Quark" cheesecake recipes. It's our favorite. It uses Quark, which you can only buy in German ethnic food shops. I tried Ricotta as a substitute, and although it's not quite the same, it's close to the original taste, although a bit too soft. This variation is very light, not filling and quite different from the traditional American cheesecake.

Ingredients:

Short pastry:
2/3 cups (150g) all-purpose flour
1 tsp baking powder
1 egg
1/3 cup (75 g) sugar
1/3 cup (75 g) margarine or unsalted butter
1 tsp vanilla extract + 1 tsp sugar (or 1 package Vanillezucker)

Filling:
1 lb quark (substitute ricotta if necessary)
3 eggs, separated
1 cup vegetable oil
2/3 cup (150g) sugar
1 package Jello French Vanilla pudding
1 tsp baking powder
1 cup (¼ l) sour cream
1 cup of light raisins, dusted with flour before use, so that they don't sink to the bottom

Preparation:

Mix dry ingredients together, add egg yolks, margarine or butter, and vanilla extract + sugar and blend carefully. Form a ball, wrap in foil and refrigerate for 15 minutes. Grease 9" springform pan and set aside.

Dust raisins with flour and beat egg whites until stiff peaks form. Blend all other filling ingredients carefully, fold in raisins, and then, with a spatula, very carefully and slowly, fold in beaten egg whites, and blend well. Place pastry in a springform pan and carefully spread over bottom and up the side (1 inch high.) Pour in the filling; the amount should fit very nicely. Bake at 350°F 50-60 minutes, or until a wooden toothpick inserted into the middle of the cake comes out clean. Turn off oven, open it a crack, and let cake cool in oven. Don't remove cake until it is cool. Otherwise, it may collapse — which wouldn't affect the taste, just the looks.

Special dish of the month: Erbsensuppe (split pea soup)

At every Kirmes (Carnival) or Schuetzenfest or Karneval (the German version of Mardi Gras,) this dish cannot be missed. Schuetzenfest is a festivity highly celebrated by the local brotherhoods, especially in the Rhineland. It goes back to Napoleon's times when it was prohibited to wear firearms. The locals decided to mock the oppressors by forming Schuetzenvereine (brotherhoods,) wearing wooden rifles and holding yearly shooting competitions. Erbsensuppe is served from big kettles, called "Gulaschkanone" (goulash cannon,) an expression created by soldiers for their huge kettles containing their daily soups. On big events, the Erbsensuppe is ladled into a deep dish, topped with a Frankfurter sausage and is just simply delicious. This picture shows such a "Gulaschkanone" used during the Karneval parades. And it is always accompanied by an "Altbier," the Düsseldorf beer specialty.

In the old days, this soup was (at least for me) a pain to prepare. The peas had to be soaked overnight, which was cumbersome. Today I use canned, or frozen peas and life is good.

So, here's the traditional version as well as the shortcut I used, to cook this delight. It's a good, hearty winter dish, what we call "soul food" in Minnesota.

Preparation: 12 hours (overnight)   Cooking time: 4 hours. The beverage for this soup should be a nice cool beer.

Ingredients (serves 12):

16 ounces (500g) dried split peas
2 quarts (2 liters) water
1 big ham bone, 1 pork knuckle or 4 pig's feet with lots of meat
4 medium size potatoes, peeled and cut into 1"cubes
2 carrots, peeled and cut into ¼" slices
1 bunch of soup greens (1 carrot, sprig of parsley, ¼ celeriac and 1 leek,) julienned
Salt
Pepper
½ cup (100g) thickly sliced bacon
1 medium sized yellow onion
Optional: 4 Frankfurters

Preparation:

Wash peas and soak in cold water to soften overnight. The next morning, add the meat. Over low heat, bring to a boil and simmer 2 – 3 hours until peas are soft. Test in between to find the right moment to add the veggies.

When peas are almost done (about ½ hour before the end of cooking time,) add vegetables and cook for another ½ hour. When soup is done, remove bones from soup, cut meat from bones and put meat back into the soup. Add pepper and salt to taste.

In a separate pan over medium heat, brown the bacon and then fry the onions in the bacon drippings. Cook until onions are transparent, then set aside.

Note: In the U.S. I have discovered the beauty of a crockpot (slow cooker,) which allows me to skip the overnight soaking of the peas. Peas, meat, and veggies are all cooked together. Here is how it's done: Take all the ingredients, except the Frankfurters, and cook on LOW for 12 hours, or on HIGH for 6 hours. Heat Frankfurters on the side. Serve.

If you opt for the additional Frankfurter (delicious, usually a feast for children,) simmer in boiling water until done.

Divide soup into 4 dishes, sprinkle with bacon and onions, add Frankfurters and serve.

Note: This soup is served with Schwarzbrot, a very dense dark bread that is "indigenous" to the Northern German states. Schwarzbrot accompanies this soup served with or without butter spread on it.

If you can't find Schwarzbrot, our American Pumpernickel is very good with this soup as well.

Too much hassle to do the overnight job? Here's the short version.

Instead of doing all this overnight preparation, use 16 ounces of canned or frozen peas instead of dried peas. I usually start to cook the veggies for a few minutes before I add the peas, and everything else works just fine.

And I have found numerous crock-pot recipes for a split pea soup. If you combine the ingredients of this recipe and the preparation methods of the crock-pot recipes, it should work very nicely.

Schwarzbrot (dark whole rye bread)

In Germany the famous Schwarzbrot, a very dark, firm whole grain rye bread, is served with or without butter.

Ingredients
3 cups + 4 Tbsp (500 g) cracked rye flour
3 cups + 4 Tbsp (500 g) cracked wheat flour
4½ + 2 Tbsp cups (750 g) all-purpose flour
1 cake fresh yeast or 1 package active dry yeast
1 Tbsp honey
3 Tbsp molasses
1 quart + 1 cup (1¼ l) warm water, divided
2 Tbsp salt
3 Tbsp ground cumin
1 Tbsp fennel seeds
1 cup nuts (walnuts, hazelnuts, etc) and/or seeds (sunflower seeds) to taste

Preparation
Mix yeast with honey, molasses and ¼ cup warm water in a big bowl. Dust with 3 cups flour and let rise for about 20 minutes in a warm (120°F) place.

Add the rest of ingredients and blend well. Pour into a big enough bread baking pan. Place in cold oven, set temperature of oven to 335°F and after the temperature is at 335°F, bake for 3 hours. Remove from oven, take out of the baking pan, and let cool inside the oven. Leave oven a slight crack open. Let rest for 2 days before serving. Is best served with butter and delicious with cheese.

Note: Don't be tempted to preheat the oven. It is important to place the mixture in the cold oven. It is also best to wait for 2 days before cutting the bread, as hard as that may be, because it smells so-o-o-o delicious!

March in Berlin

Berlin, German Capital, Brandenburg Gate

March in Berlin

Berlin is a magic word in Germany. Its history as a major capital city goes back to 1470. Under the electoral princes the country thrived. Around the end of the 17th century, the Huguenots from France (a Protestant sect) were given asylum, so their French names are often found in this region. Later, Berlin became the capital of the Prussian kingdom under famous King Frederic the Great, and consequently the capital of the Holy Roman Empire under Emperor Wilhelm and Bismarck, his Chancellor. After World War I, it was the capital of the first German Republic, and later on, before and during WWII, the capital of Nazi Germany.

From its early days on, Berlin was a center of political and intellectual power. It was the center of German culture, arts, fashion and "Savoir Vivre" – a wonderful way of life. Berlin's people (German: the Berliner) have always been renowned for their witty, sharp, and dry kind of humor, their very down-to-earth attitudes toward their rulers. Even their dialect, called Berliner Schnauze (the "Berlin Snout",) is famous throughout Germany.

After World War II, though, Berlin was a divided city, its Eastern part was the capital of the Eastern German Democratic Republic while Bonn became the capital of the Federal Republic of Germany. And where West Berlin was already a thriving center, once again, of survival and culture, East Berlin was a gray, colorless city. However, the dream of a united Berlin as the capital of a united Germany never ceased to be part of German politics, and in 1989 the dream came true. When the wall fell, and the Brandenburg Gate was reopened, and the public could walk from West to East Berlin, the nation was delirious with joy.

Today you find theaters, museums, and churches reopened, and the "old quarters," like the Nikolaiviertel, have been restored to their old glory.

Pictures from top right clockwise: Deutscher Dom, Chancellor "White House," Sony Center, Old Berlin, Reichstag, street musicians, Reichstag atrium with view of the Parliament chamber below, area maps of Berlin and Brandenburg

Berlin and the beautiful state of Brandenburg are now a paradise for tourists with all its culture, restaurants, parks, and markets, and a walk along the Spree and the Havel rivers is always fun.

Berlin is also proof that old and modern can mix well. The old "Reichstag," the parliament building, has been restored on the outside to its old glory. The inside, however, is a modern building with a walkway around the central glass pillar, which depicts the history of Germany, and Berlin. The new "Kanzleramt," German's "White House," is very modern, called "The bungalow." The new Sony Center on Potsdamer Platz in previous East Berlin is the best example of the way the new Berlin is developing at a breathtaking speed. We liked the old-fashioned neighborhoods around the French and German Dome, with musicians and leisure, old houses and pubs and restaurants. The new shopping malls around Potsdamer Platz reminded us strongly of the Mall of America – a seemingly endless, no-fuss, "shop 'til you drop" area. And since the German administration moved to Berlin, the city has become a magnet for major corporate companies from all over the world.

About the Menu

A traditional German dinner menu (dinner here being the big meal served at Americans' lunch time) is still today traditionally preceded by a nice, light, mostly clear soup. If you look at German menus, you will always find a selection of soups as well as appetizers and salads.

I grew up with these clear bouillons, usually enriched by adding little dumplings, flaked eggs, or "Pfannekuchen" (the German pancakes) cut into strips, These soups are very light, just enough to open the palate and prepare the stomach for the delicacies to come.

Traditional German menus serve the salad with the main dish as a side salad rather than serving the salad before the meal.

I am not sure that sweet rice is a traditional American dessert, but in Germany this is a part of fine dining, using round rice. (I used Arborio, and it worked well) In Germany this rice is called "Milchreis" (milk rice) and is cooked in milk or wine and served with fruit, or cinnamon and sugar, or whipped cream

March in Berlin

Appetizer:
Fennel salad with orange-caper dressing

Soup:
Clear beef bouillon with pancake strips

Entrée:
Chicken ragout à la Berlin with rice and carrots

Side salad:
Iceberg lettuce with almond lemon dressing

Dessert:
Sweet rice in red wine with whipped cream

Beverage:
Riesling white wine

Special dish of the month:
Tafelspitz (Horseradish Loin,) cooked beef with horseradish and chives cream

A nice leftover dish:
Tafelspitz Salad

Appetizer: Fennel salad with orange-caper dressing

Ingredients (serves 4):
4 medium-size fennel bulbs, cleaned and halved
1 bunch green onions, including most of the green, cleaned and julienned
2 tomatoes, skinned, seeded and julienned

Dressing:
4 Tbsp oil
4 Tbsp vinegar
½ cup white wine
Juice of 1 orange
¼ cup of capers
½ bunch parsley, chives and mint leaves, finely chopped
4 sprigs of parsley (cut stems short)
2 hard-boiled eggs, cooled and chopped
Salt and pepper to taste
1 pinch sugar

Preparation:
Bring salted water to a boil and blanch fennel bulbs for about 10 minutes; drain and set aside to cool. When cool, cut bulbs into strips, place on serving plates and top with tomatoes and then green onions.

For dressing, mix oil and vinegar with white wine and orange juice. Add capers and finely chopped herbs, and mix well. Add the chopped eggs and pepper, salt and sugar to taste. Pour over salad shortly before serving and garnish each dish with a sprig of parsley.

Soup: Clear beef bouillon with pancake strips

Ingredients (serves 4):
1½ lbs beef soup bones and beef ribs each
1 lb marrow bone
4 quarts cold water
1 parsley root, or 1 bunch of parsley
2 sprigs of thyme
1 bay leaf
2 big carrots, peeled and diced
½ celery root (celeriac,) peeled and diced
3 onions, peeled and diced
Onion peels (they give a wonderful color)
1 leek, cleaned and cut into rings
4 Tbsp vegetable oil
2 leafy ends of celery stalks

To clear soup:
3 egg whites beaten to soft peaks
1 carrot, peeled and diced
2 Tbsp vegetable oil

Preparation:
Put meat, bones and onion peels in a large pot, cover with cold water, and bring slowly to a boil. Remove froth that develops and keep simmering. Meanwhile, in a separate pot, heat oil and sauté diced vegetables until onions are transparent. Add parsley, thyme, bay leaf and roasted vegetables to meat. Cover and simmer for about 5 hours. To clear soup, cover a colander or sieve with cheesecloth and pour soup through it. Add beaten egg whites to soup and stir until they become a firm mass. Add carrot and oil and stir until all is firm. Pour through the sieve covered with cheesecloth again. The bouillon should have a clear consistency now.

Note: If you don't have the time to do all this, there are good, ready-made bouillons available on the market. I believe natural/organic beef broths have the best flavor.

Pfannekuchenstreifen (pancake strips)

Ingredients (serves 4):
1 cup all-purpose flour
Pinch salt
1 cup milk
1 egg
2 Tbsp vegetable oil and 1 Tbsp butter

Preparation:
Combine flour and salt, then stir in milk, and then stir in egg, and blend until smooth.

In a flat pan (like a tortilla pan,) bring oil and butter to medium heat. Spoon just enough batter into the pan to make a very flat pancake. Brown on one side, then close cover and fry until firm. Turn pancake onto a flat board and prick bubbles with a toothpick. Repeat until all pancakes are done.

Roll pancakes up, one at a time, cut into thin strips, and add to soup before serving.

Filled Pancake Strips, a nice appetizer

These pancakes can also be filled with all sorts of spreads, mashed salmon, marinated salmon or whatever you fancy. Roll them up, fix them with toothpicks 1 inch apart, and slice them so that each toothpick becomes the center of a slice. Serve on a few lettuce leaves and serve with white wine.

Entrée: Chicken ragout à la Berlin with rice

Ingredients (serves 4):
1 or 2 Stewing chickens (about 4 lbs,) cut into pieces
1 calf tongue (optional)
1 calf sweetbread (optional)
1 onion
1 bay leaf
1 Tbsp black peppercorns
1 bunch of soup veggies consisting of 1 carrot, 1 leek, ¼ celeriac and 2 sprigs parsley or a parsley root, if you can find it

For the Sauce:
½ - 1 lb asparagus cut into 1" pieces (white if you can find it, otherwise green)
1 cup sliced mushrooms
½ cup fresh morels (or 3 dried morels, soaked in water for ½ hour)
1 Tbsp Butter and 2 Tbsp lemon juice for the mushrooms
4 Tbsp butter
4 Tbsp flour
2 cups chicken broth
½ cup asparagus water
½ cup white wine
1 tsp lemon juice or more to taste
1 pinch of lemon zest or to taste
1 pinch each pepper and salt to taste
1 dash Worcestershire sauce to taste
1 egg yolk
1 cup half & half

For the puff pastry half-moons:
1 leaf puff pastry (thawed)

Preparation:
Prepare meat first. In a deep pot, cover chicken, tongue, sweetbread, soup veggies, peppercorns, bay leaf, and onion with cold water and bring to a boil. Reduce heat and simmer for about 1½ hours. Take out sweetbread after 20 minutes and tongue after 1 hour.

When chicken is done, skin chicken and cut into strips. Dut tongue into slices, and dice sweetbread. Set aside and keep warm, while you cook asparagus and mushrooms.

Cook asparagus in a small amount of water, adding a pinch of salt and sugar, and 1 tsp butter, until asparagus is al dente. Drain and save water for sauce. Sauté mushrooms in butter and lemon juice. Sauté morels in 1 Tbsp butter.

To make puff pastry half-moons for decoration:
Preheat oven to 350°F, cut puff pastry into 12 half-moons (3 per person,) and bake for about 15 min., or until they are nicely golden brown.

To make sauce:
In a pot, melt butter and stir in flour until blended. Add chicken broth, asparagus water, and white wine, and stir until it's well blended and has a creamy consistency. Add asparagus pieces and mushrooms. Add lemon juice and zest to taste. (The sauce should not be too tart.) Add pepper and salt and a dash of Worcester¬shire sauce. Heat until sauce is hot but doesn't boil. Combine egg yolk with the half & half, remove sauce from heat and carefully blend in the egg/cream mixture. Add meat to sauce and heat, but make sure the sauce doesn't start boiling again.

Serve the ragout in a flat bowl, topped with the puff pastry pieces and a little portion of chopped parsley. It can be garnished with a tablespoon of capers. Serve with white rice.

If you'd like to serve this dish with a side of vegetables, I'd suggest you serve steamed carrots.

Note: On Sundays, this dish was usually served with crab meat and crab tails.

Note: Any leftover chicken broth was used to make a wonderful soup, by adding different kinds of vegetables, semolina dumplings, or chicken livers, hearts and stomachs. Sounds funny to American ears? I grew up with ragouts made with these ingredients, and they were really good.

Vegetables could be a combination of snap peas, carrots and cauliflower.

Semolina dumplings are easily made: Combine 1 cup of semolina, 1 egg and a pinch of salt. Mix well, with two spoons form into dumplings, and simmered in the soup until done. I have sometimes just added noodles.

Beverage: Riesling white wine

Side Salad: Iceberg lettuce with almond lemon dressing

Ingredients (serves 4):
1 head of iceberg lettuce
4 Tbsp chopped almonds

For the dressing:
6 Tbsp almond oil
4 Tbsp lemon juice, freshly squeezed
2 Tbsp water
Pepper and salt to taste

Tear lettuce leaves into small pieces, or cut into strips. Mix dressing ingredients and pour over lettuce. Carefully toss lettuce with dressing to coat all leaves.

Serve on salad plates and garnish with chopped the almonds.

Note: I like to use sea salt, which has a more distinct taste than normal salt. I found out that with lemon juice, you need to use more salt so the dressing is not so acidic; salt mellows the acidic taste of the lemon.

Dessert: Sweet rice in red wine with whipped cream (Reisflammeri)

Ingredients (serves 4):
1 cup (250 g) round rice like the Italian Arborio
1 quart (1 l) red wine (my preference is red Zinfandel)
1 pinch salt
2 Tbsp (40 g) butter
1 zest from lemon
2 cloves
½ tsp ground cinnamon
2/3 cups (150 g) sugar, or less, depending on the wine's taste
½ cup (1/8 l) heavy whipping cream
2 Tbsp (40g) sugar

Preparation:
Wash rice and put into a deep pot. Add red wine, salt, butter, lemon zest, cloves, and cinnamon. Bring to a boil, reduce heat, and simmer on low heat for about 30 – 40 minutes, or until red wine has been absorbed. Add sugar to taste and stir carefully. If the rice doesn't seem to be fully cooked, add more wine and simmer until rice is soft.

Rinse a glass bowl with cold water and pour rice into the bowl. Use a wet spoon to smooth the surface. Let cool.

After rice has cooled, turn over onto a serving plate.

Beat whipping cream with sugar. Garnish rice with a bit of the whipped cream.

Serve the rice and pass the rest of the whipped cream.

Special dish of the month: Meerrettichlende (or Tafelspitz,) beef loin with horseradish and chives cream

Tafelspitz is the most well-known name for this dish, which is a local dish in most European areas. The preparation varies slightly from country to country. In Berlin, it is called "Meerrettichlende" (translated "Horseradish Loin".) In Austria, its preparation includes a horseradish-apple sauce called "Apfel Kren." It is served with carrots and boiled potatoes, or potato salad, or fried potatoes, depending upon where you go. Our favorite place in Vienna to order this dish was the city's oldest restaurant, the "Griechenbeisl," in the old part of Vienna.

In cookbooks, I found as many variations as there are regions in Germany, but this is the version I found in Berlin. I also think that a ready-made horseradish cream is as good as freshly ground horseradish mixed with cream. The fruit you'd add in Germany is called "Preisselbeeren." Our cranberries come closest to that taste, although some German recipes call for red currant jelly instead of cranberries.

Ingredients (serves 4):
1½ lbs beef loin
2 Tbsp vegetable oil mixed with a pinch each of pepper and salt
½ cup butter
2 medium sized onions, thinly sliced
1 cup hot bouillon or beef broth
2 tart apples, peeled and diced
1 Tbsp butter
4 Tbsp grated horseradish
1 Tbsp medium hot mustard (preferably Dijon)
1 Tbsp flour
4 Tbsp sour cream
2 Tbsp cooked cranberries
Lemon juice to taste

Preparation
Wash beef, pat dry. Rub with the mixture of oil, pepper and salt. In a pan over medium heat, melt ½ cup butter and brown beef on all sides. Add onions and cook until transparent. Slowly add hot broth and simmer over medium heat for about 40 minutes.

While beef is cooking, sauté diced apples in 1 Tbsp butter until medium soft. Stir flour into sour cream, add horseradish, mustard and apples and – 2 minutes before the end of the 40 minutes – add this mixture to the meat. Stir carefully. Add cranberries or red currant jelly and lemon juice to taste. Simmer for another 2 minutes and serve.

Note: The beef is served in its broth in a deep dish with the chives cream served on the side. Side dishes are steamed potatoes and a cucumber salad. As a beverage, I prefer a Riesling. However, my dad would only allow a light beer, like Pilsner.

Here are the two traditional sauces that go with boiled beef, chives cream, (being part of this recipe) and apple-horseradish cream. Both sauces are a traditional part of the Austrian Tafelspitz, and my family used to serve the chives cream with steamed or baked potatoes. Yummmy!

Chives cream

Ingredients (serves 4):
4.5 ounces (120 g) white bread or roll
warm water to soak bread
6 hard-boiled egg yolks
dash white vinegar
6 Tbsp vegetable oil
pinch each of salt, pepper, sugar
2 Tbsp finely chopped chives.

Preparation:
Cut the crust off the roll or bread, soak in warm water, then squeeze dry. Finely mash the egg yolks and mix with the bread. Gradually stir in oil, vinegar, and seasonings. Add water until the sauce is smooth and slightly thickened. Add chives, and blend well.

Apple Horseradish Sauce (Apfelkren)

Ingredients:
2 large apples, peeled, cored and grated
1 Tbsp sugar
1 Tbsp shredded or ground horseradish
1 tsp white vinegar
1 pinch each salt and pepper

Preparation:
Mix grated apples and horseradish together. Stir in all the other ingredients and blend thoroughly. Also goes well with ham or fish.

A nice leftover dish: Tafelspitz salad

Since my mother was called the "Leftover Queen," she took great pride in adopting recipes like this from wherever she would go. I got this recipe from our friend Ruth in Germany, who got it from the chef of "Haus Stemberg" in Neviges, the town next to my hometown of Langenberg.

Ingredients (serves 4):
1 quart cooked leftover Tafelspitz (boiled beef,) thinly sliced
2 small red onions, thinly sliced
1 leek, thinly sliced
1 Tbsp chives, cut into thin rolls
2 hard boiled eggs, finely chopped
3 Tbsp oil (olive oil is best)
2 Tbsp balsamic vinegar or red wine vinegar
Salt and pepper to taste
1 tsp mustard (I prefer Dijon)
4 lettuce leaves
4 Tbsp finely chopped parsley
4 cherry tomatoes, quartered

Preparation:
Blanch leek slices in boiling water. Remove and quickly dip and then cool in cold water. Mix beef, leek, and onion.

In a large bowl, combine oil, vinegar, salt, pepper and mustard. Add beef, onions, leek, eggs and chives, and toss gently.

Using dinner plates, put a lettuce leaf on each plate, and top with the salad mixture. Garnish with chopped parsley (1 Tbsp for each dish) and the cherry tomatoes.

This salad is best served with crispy, warm French bread and a nice cool wine like Chardonnay, or a beer.

April in the Bergische Land

Town of Burg, typical for the Bergische Land region of the Rhineland

April in the Bergische Land

This area is, where my heart is because it is my "home region." I grew up in the picturesque city of Langenberg, and every time I go back I fall in love again. I love every inch of it with its quaint half-timber houses, typical slate roofs and sidings, and crooked cobblestone streets.

The Bergische Land is a hilly area with deep narrow valleys and elevations up to 3,000 feet. However dedicated I am to the place of my birth, I have to admit it: all the old towns in this area have the same "Langenberg" charm.

This region has a history going back about 1,000 years. Around 1100, the Counts of Berg emerged as its most powerful dynasty of rulers (thus the name "Bergisches Land," "land of the Berg Dynasty".) In 1280, the Count of Berg moved his residence from Schloss Burg to Düsseldorf, and 100 years later the Count was elevated to Duke. Today, their medieval castle, Schloss Burg, is a museum where tourists can learn about life in the Middle Ages. This castle is well preserved and worth a family trip. In the castle chapel (Schlosskapelle,) you'd probably find a musical or company event, or a wedding ceremony – events, which has to be booked a year ahead of time!

The Bergisches Land was the industrial center for manufacturers of fabrics, yarns, needles, and everything else needed by the clothing industry. Langenberg became wealthy with its needle industry, neighboring Wuppertal with yarns and cloth, and Solingen is still today world famous for its silverware and cutlery. The Klingenmuseum (the blade museum) in Solingen is worth a trip, as well as the town of Solingen itself.

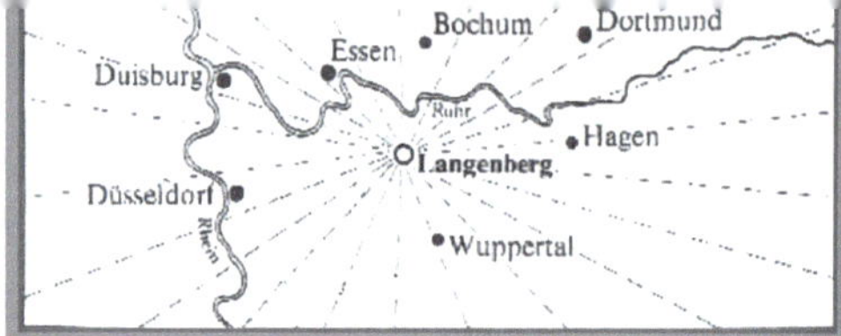

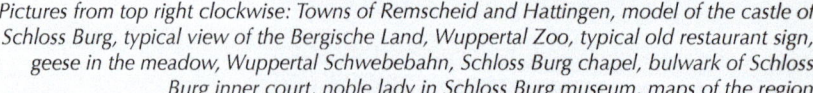

Pictures from top right clockwise: Towns of Remscheid and Hattingen, model of the castle of Schloss Burg, typical view of the Bergische Land, Wuppertal Zoo, typical old restaurant sign, geese in the meadow, Wuppertal Schwebebahn, Schloss Burg chapel, bulwark of Schloss Burg inner court, noble lady in Schloss Burg museum, maps of the region

Tourists love this area for its recreational value, and hikers take long tours through the woods to quaint family restaurants like "Schmal am Schmalen" in Langenberg. It's just one of many of its kind, but one of my favorites. Boaters find large dammed lakes, city people find nature, hikers find well-organized hiking trails, and they all find cafes in forests and towns with outside seating, waffles with cherries and cream, and delicious coffee.

Wuppertal, another major city in this area, also has one of Germany's most beautiful zoos, and it has the Schwebebahn, the suspended railway. This train has been in service for now more than 100 years, and is still the No. 1 public transportation in this very narrow valley, following the Wupper river that flows through the whole city.

Do you wonder what all those white dots are in that picture of a meadow? They're geese, the "turkeys" for Germany's traditional holiday kitchen. On November 10, St. Martin's Day, the family enjoys a goose with apple and prune stuffing, red cabbage, and dumplings, and this is where farmers raise them!

About the Menu

Langenberg is where I was born and raised until I was seven years old. And I still go back and enjoy this unique little town, with its old houses and narrow streets.

The menu for this month is what my mom would serve on special days, with a tongue of beef or preferably veal being one of the most delicate kinds of meat you can find.

Cold sweet fruit soup (Kaltschale) is a specialty we often had as children, especially in spring and summer. You can make them with basically any fruit. Try and replace the strawberries in our recipe with any fruit you fancy, like peaches, cherries, or raspberries, and enjoy. And of course, there are several different local recipes with or without buttermilk, but the basics are always the same. And on a trip to Hungary we found out this dish is a favorite national appetizer!

The haddock fillets are a memory from our Friday meals, and I especially love this mustard cream, that complements the fine haddock taste so well.

April in the Bergische Land

Appetizer:
Butter beans salad

Soup:
Creamed potato soup with leek

Entrée:
Ragout of calf tongue with a cauliflower side dish

Side salad:
Romaine lettuce with creamy mustard dressing and walnuts

Dessert:
Cold sweet strawberry soup (Erdbeerkaltschale)

Beverage:
Chardonnay or Pinot Grigio

Special dish of the month:
Haddock fillets in creamy mustard sauce baked with vegetable julienne and served with steamed potatoes

Appetizer: Butter Beans salad

Ingredients (serves 4):
2 cans butter beans, drained (but reserve some of the water)
1 red onion, finely sliced
½ red bell pepper, finely chopped
4 leaves of green lettuce
For the vinaigrette:
⅓ cup oil (I like grapeseed oil, but any good oil will do)
¼ cup white wine vinegar
freshly ground black pepper to taste
salt to taste
2 Tbsp parsley, finely chopped
1 Tbsp basil, finely chopped

Preparation:
Mix butter beans, onions, and bell peppers carefully.

In a separate bowl, mix vinaigrette together. Pour over beans and blend well.

Place one leaf of lettuce on each plate and spoon one portion of bean salad on top. Sprinkle with chopped parsley. Use a sprig of parsley as a garnish. Serve with crisp white or whole wheat bread.

Note: Of course, in the old days, these beans had to be cooked from scratch, but I am going to spare us the effort. The canned beans we can buy today are just as good.

Soup: Creamed potato soup with leek julienne

Ingredients (serves 4):
12 medium sized potatoes, diced to ½" pieces
4 strips bacon
3 cups hot chicken broth
1 cup of milk
white pepper, salt to taste
½ large leek washed and julienne cut, including ¼ of the green
1 Tbsp butter
4 Tbsp parsley, finely chopped

Preparation:
Heat deep pan over medium-high heat. Add bacon and cook until crisp. Remove bacon, but leave bacon fat in a pan. Break bacon into pieces and set aside.

Add potatoes to bacon fat. Stir and cook for about 5 minutes. Add broth and milk, cover and cook until potatoes are done (about another 5-10 minutes.) Remove half of the potatoes and thoroughly.

Return to the soup and add bacon. Add pepper and salt to taste, stir and bring to a boil, and then remove soup from heat immediately.

While the potatoes are cooking, sauté leek in butter over medium heat. When the soup is ready to serve, stir in leek

Ladle soup into 4 bowls, sprinkle with chopped parsley, and serve with fresh, warm French bread or whole wheat or rye bread.

Note: I love to add one carrot, julienne cut and roasted, to this recipe. It is not the way it's supposed to be — but it tastes so-o-o good! Leek needs to be cleaned very carefully, see also note in Ingredients.

Entrée: Ragout from calf tongue with a side dish of cauliflower baked in puff pastry

Ingredients (serves 4):
2 lbs calf tongue
½ leek washed
1 carrot, peeled
¼ celery root (celeriac,) peeled
1 tsp salt
1 tsp white peppercorns
1 bay leaf
1 Tbsp butter
1 Tbsp flour
10-15 capers
1 Tbsp white wine (like Chardonnay or Pinot Grigio)
dash lemon juice or to taste
4 cups of broth from the cooked tongue

Preparation:
Wash tongue carefully, with cold water, bring to a boil in a large saucepan and bring to a boil. When water comes to a boil, there will be some froth; skim it off with a spoon and discard it. Now add other ingredients (vegetables, pep¬per corns, salt, bay leaf) and cook over medium heat for 1 to 1½ hours, depending on the size of the tongue. The tongue is done when the tip of the tongue is soft. Remove from heat. Skin tongue and set aside. In a medium pan, melt butter over medium heat, and add flour constantly stirring until flour is dissolved. Add 4 cups of broth and keep stirring until you have a creamy consistency. Add wine, lemon juice, and capers, stirring constantly. Cut tongue into thick slices, add to the sauce and set aside for a few minutes before serving.

Note: You can also serve this entrée with broccoli, Brussels sprouts, cauliflower or kohlrabi, and potatoes or rice.

Another option is this: when using beef tongue instead of calf tongue, the recipe would be the same. However, the sauce should be made with red wine instead of white wine, and instead of capers, finely chopped onions, thyme, and black pepper should be used for the sauce.

Side dish: Cauliflower baked in puff pastry

Ingredients (serves 4):
1 package of puff pastry
1 cauliflower, washed, and broken into flowerets
1 cup (200 g) shredded cheddar cheese

For the sauce:
1 cup of yogurt
1 cup white wine
2 eggs
salt and white pepper to taste
pinch nutmeg
1 cup vegetable broth
Breadcrumbs if necessary

Preparation:
Preheat oven to 400°F (200°C)

Blanch cauliflower for 5 minutes. Roll out puff pastry according to directions and place in a 9" baking pan. Sprinkle with cheese. Add cauliflower. Mix ingredients for the sauce, and pour over the cauliflower.

Bake at 400°F for about 40 – 45 minutes; the dish should be nicely brown on top.

Note: If you think the sauce is too thin, add some breadcrumbs.

Beverage: White wine like Chardonnay or Pinot Grigio
I find it's best to use the same wine for the sauce that I serve with the meal.

Leftover Special: Calf tongue salad with mushrooms

Got leftovers from the calf tongue ragout? Try this:

Mix 1 cup (1/4 l) of cooking broth (reserved from cooking the tongue) with 1 Tbsp honey, 1 Tbsp Bavarian mustard, 2 Tbsp white vinegar, salt, ground white pepper to taste, and 3 Tbsp sunflower seed oil, to form a not-too-thin vinaigrette. Marinate the thinly sliced tongue and set aside.

Peel 6 shallots. Peel 1 glove of garlic. Heat 2 Tbsp vegetable oil and cook shallots over medium heat. Add 2/3 cup port wine, 1 sprig rosemary, and a garlic clove. Sauté for about 20 minutes or until shallots are tender. Remove rosemary and garlic and add 2 Tbsp cold butter.

In a separate saucepan, sauté 8 medium sized mushrooms, cut in halves, in 2 Tbsp butter, until mushrooms are tender. Arrange tongue on a salad platter. Spoon vinaigrette over tongue slices. Sprinkle mushrooms over this and top with shallots. Garnish with chives rings. Serve with dark rye bread, or French bread.

Side salad: Romaine lettuce with creamy mustard dressing and walnuts

Ingredients (serves 4):
8 ounces (225 g) young Romaine lettuce
1 hard-boiled, egg, chopped
½ cup chopped walnuts
½ small red onion, finely chopped
4 sprigs of fresh parsley for garnish
For the dressing:
3 Tbsp walnut oil
1½ Tbsp lemon juice or to taste
1 Tbsp Dijon mustard
½ cup sour cream
1 Tbsp water
Salt and pepper to taste

Preparation:
Wash lettuce and dry thoroughly. In a large bowl, mix lettuce with walnuts and onion. In a separate bowl, mix oil, lemon juice, sour cream, mustard, and pepper and salt to taste. Pour over salad and toss gently. Serve on 4 salad plates, top with chopped eggs and garnish with a sprig of fresh parsley.

Dessert: Cold sweet strawberry soup (Erdbeerkaltschale)

Ingredients (serves 4):
2 cups (500 ml) buttermilk
1 cup (125 g) whipping cream
1 cup (125 g) yogurt
2 ½ lbs (600 g) strawberries
4 Tbsp honey
juice of ½ lemon
1 tsp vanilla extract
1 cup chopped almonds, lightly roasted

Preparation:
Wash strawberries and remove green stems. Mix buttermilk, yogurt, vanilla extract, honey, lemon juice and about half of the strawberries in a large bowl or mixer and puree thoroughly. Refrigerate. Set aside 4 strawberries. Cut rest of strawberries in halves. Whip cream until stiff, and carefully mix with strawberry halves. Just before serving, stir into buttermilk puree. Portion into 4 bowls, sprinkle with almonds and garnish with one strawberry each.

Alternative recipe: Another way to prepare this dessert is to mix 2 lbs strawberries with 1 pinch cinnamon, 1 Tbsp lemon juice and 1 Tbsp sugar. Blend until smooth and refrigerate for 2 hours. Ladle into 4 bowls, sprinkle with chopped mint leaves and dabs of whipped cream. Serve cold and enjoy. Great for hot summer days.

Special dish of the month: Haddock fillets in creamy mustard sauce baked with vegetable julienne

Haddock is a fish that is one of the May treats in Germany, just like white asparagus, new potatoes, and the first strawberries. In my family, haddock was always served with these new potatoes and a creamy mustard sauce. The fancy vegetable julienne came later as an additional variation; when I grew up there were only straight, no fuss carrots and potatoes served with the fish.

Ingredients (serves 4):
4 medium-sized fillets of haddock
Pinch of salt
3 Tbsp butter, preferably unsalted.
4 quarts (1 l) water
1½ lbs small potatoes, peeled, or new potatoes, brushed
3 carrots, peeled, and julienned
1 leek, washed, dried, and julienned
¼ celery root (celeriac,) peeled, and julienned
1 Tbsp flour
1 cup (250 ml) milk
1 cup hot broth (either fish, vegetable or chicken broth)
Pinch of ground nutmeg
1 – 2 Tbsp mustard (Dijon or Grey Poupon,) to taste
Pepper and salt
2 Tbsp chopped fresh or 1½ dried dill

Preparation:
Preheat oven to 400°F (200°C)

Rinse fish, pat dry, and salt (just a little.) Grease a baking dish with 1 Tbsp butter and place fish in dish. In a large pot, bring enough salted water to a boil to blanch the julienned vegetables for about 2 minutes. Drain and sprinkle vegetables evenly over the fish fillets. Cover with aluminum foil, and bake for 15 minutes. In the meantime, steam potatoes until done.

In a saucepan, melt 1 Tbsp butter and stir in flour until well blended. Add broth and milk, constantly stirring until medium thick. Simmer for another 10 minutes, and season with nutmeg, mustard, salt and pepper.

In a separate saucepan, melt 1 Tbsp butter, add potatoes and dill, and toss carefully.

To serve, spoon sauce on 4 dinner plates and place fish fillets topped with vegetables on top. Place potatoes on side and garnish with a small sprig of dill. Serve with a small cucumber salad with a dill yogurt dressing or a dill lemon dressing.

A beer or crisp white wine like Pinot Grigio goes well with this dish.

Note: If you cannot find haddock, another white fish would do as well. Since it's always fun to "eat" with the eyes, I choose vegetables that not only compliment the taste of the fish and mustard sauce. I also create a colorful "picture." In this dish, I would place the carrots and leek, and the white fish on top of the golden sauce giving it a nice contrast to the green parsley we use for garnish.

Instead of steaming the potatoes separately, you can also julienne them and sprinkle them over the haddock together with the other vegetable julienne. It saves time, and the taste is just as good.

And if you don't want to do the julienne of vegetables, steamed broccoli or carrots are a good substitute.

May in Osnabrück

Old Town Osnabrück

May in Osnabrück

Osnabrück, with its massive, still-intact old wall, the more than 1000-year-old cathedral and the marketplace, is a city with an important history in Europe. Charlemagne founded the town around 780, and Osnabrück became one of the oldest bishoprics (seats of bishops) in Europe. Around 900 the Emperor granted the town merchant, customs, and coinage rights, but it took another 250 years to acquire city rights (the right to erect fortifications.) The city walls you see today were erected around that time. Osnabrück then became a member of the merchant league "Hanse," the Hanseatic League, which gave the city an enormous influence in medieval European trade.

When, during the time of Reformation, the rulers and citizens of Osnabrück elected to follow the Protestant movement, they created an ongoing conflict with the Catholic bishop. Europe was shaken by religious wars until the peace of Westphalia ended the Thirty Years' War in 1648. The war-faring parties held their negotiations in Osnabrück, and the peace agreement was signed here. For the city, of Osnabrueck the Westphalian Peace led to the unique regulation that the city would be governed alternatively by a Catholic and a Protestant bishop.

The city suffered severely from the bombings of WWII. Fortunately, though, it has been rebuilt to reflect the picture of the medieval city.

Today, Osnabrück is the heart of a wonderful surrounding landscape, the Osnabrücker Land. This region is located in the southern part of Lower Saxony, between Hanover to the East, Münster to the North and Dortmund to the West,

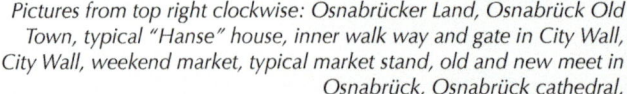

Pictures from top right clockwise: Osnabrücker Land, Osnabrück Old Town, typical "Hanse" house, inner walk way and gate in City Wall, City Wall, weekend market, typical market stand, old and new meet in Osnabrück, Osnabrück cathedral,

with a population of about 160,000. Osnabrück, as a University City, is humming with young people.

As in other cities in Germany, the bicycle is one of the main means of transportation, not sport. The area around Osnabrück is a tourist attraction for people of all ages, a paradise for bikers and hikers with long trails through meadows and along creeks. Excursions to the Teutoburg Forest and the Externsteine, a cluster of interesting rock formations, are well worth the time.

North of Osnabrück, closer to Münster and Warendorf, you find the famous German horse country. World renown horse breeders raise dressage world champions and jump and race horses for the International Championships in this area and are famous all over the world.

Culturally, Osnabrück and its surroundings are quite interesting as well. Music, art galleries, and art events are part of daily life. And cozy pubs and restaurants invite one to stay longer than one intended to.

May in Osnabrück

Appetizer:
Marinated Salmon à la Ingeborg

Soup:
Clear white asparagus soup with asparagus pieces

Entrée:
White asparagus with melted golden butter, new potatoes, and cooked ham

Side salad:
Carrot salad with sweet and sour dressing

Dessert:
Rhubarb-vanilla cream

Beverage:
White Burgundy

Special dish of the month:
Matjes (herring fillets) with fresh potatoes in a creamy sauce

About the Menu

Finally — asparagus time! Everybody was waiting for this time of the year when we could go out to the farms to get this delicacy fresh from the fields. It was always a great family trip to the Netherlands as we lived close to the border.

Anything served with asparagus other than melted butter, spring potatoes boiled in their skin, and cooked ham with a green salad, was considered barbaric (at least in my family.)

Today that's not true if you go to a restaurant. There you'll find all asparagus with hollandaise sauce or melted butter, asparagus ragout (sometimes mixed with mushrooms,) asparagus with chicken or ham, or with a Wiener Schnitzel (veal) or veal tongue. You'd have as many recipes as you have chefs!

However, the purist would have it the same way my parents used to prepare it, preceded by a cup of asparagus soup, and followed by fresh strawberries. Wonderful.

Rhubarb-vanilla cream is one of my favorites and so easy to make. The vanilla complements the tartness of the rhubarb in a terrific way.

For a beverage, white wine is not a must, the menu goes as well with a light (as opposed to a dark) beer.

Appetizer: Marinated Salmon à la Ingeborg

Ingredients (serves 4):
About 2 lbs (1 kg) salmon, cut lengthwise in half
5 tsp coarse sea salt
1 tsp juniper, grated carefully
2 tsp brown sugar
1 tsp each of lemon pepper and ground pimento (red pepper)
2 bundles of dill long stems removed
Maggi Fondor seasoning (see Note below)

Preparation:
Mix spices and brown sugar, and rub into salmon on all sides. Cover each side with dill. Add a little Fondor seasoning on each side. Lay the two slices of salmon on top of each other, first wrap them firmly in plastic wrap, and then wrap them in aluminum foil.

Place packet in a large enough bowl so it can lie flat, and place a weight on top.

Refrigerate for 1 day, checking to see if some more salt is needed. Close packet, turn over, and refrigerate for another day. (Marinating time is a total of 48 hours.) When ready to serve, place salmon on a plate and thinly slice with a sharp knife. Garnish with some sprigs of dill.

Goes well with warm, fresh French bread.

Note: Maggi Fondor is the original seasoning that my friend uses. It's available on the Internet, but can also be replaced with a pinch of celery salt and a pinch of paprika or chicken or fish seasoning mixtures.

Soup: Clear white asparagus soup with asparagus pieces

Use the reserved fresh asparagus peelings, cut-off ends and 4 reserved pieces of the asparagus entrée on the next page for this soup.

Ingredients (serves 4):
2 pints cold water
Salt, white pepper
Reserved peelings off 2 bunches of white asparagus
4 pieces of white asparagus peeled and cut into 1" pieces
1 Tbsp cold butter
½ tsp sugar
ground paprika for garnish
4 sprigs parsley stems removed

Preparation:
Put the asparagus peelings in a big pot. Add 2 pints cold water, pepper, salt, sugar and butter, and bring to a boil. Reduce heat and simmer for about 20 minutes. Pour through a sieve covered with a cheese cloth. Bring soup to a simmer again, add asparagus pieces, and simmer for another 5 minutes. Asparagus should be al dente. If necessary, add more salt and white pepper to taste.

Ladle soup into soup cups. Garnish each with a pinch of paprika. Cut stems off the parsley to garnish the soup with this parsley "flower."

Serve with French bread or golden toasted bread triangles.

Note: I normally have a container of asparagus broth from the last time I cooked asparagus in my freezer. It makes it easier and you don't have too much hassle when you're making the soup.

Entrée: White asparagus with melted golden butter, new potatoes, and sliced cooked ham

Ingredients (serves 4):
2 bunches (1,2 kg) white asparagus peeled
1 Tbsp salt
½ tsp sugar
2 Tbsp butter
8 cups (2 l) water
2-3 thin slices of cooked ham for each person
For the golden butter:
1-2 sticks of unsalted butter

Preparation:
With a sharp knife or a special asparagus peeler, peel the asparagus very thinly and cut off the woody ends of the stalks. Put 1" of water in a saucepan large enough to lay the asparagus flat on the bottom. Add salt, sugar and 2 Tbsp butter, and place asparagus in pan. Bring water to a boil, reduce heat, and simmer until asparagus is tender but still al dente (10-15 minutes.) Remove from water, and place on a pre-warmed flat serving plate. Reserve broth and set aside.

In a separate saucepan, melt sticks of butter over medium heat. Be sure that it browns nicely, but does not get too dark, or burned. You can also melt it in the microwave. Serve in a separate sauce dish, to pour over the asparagus and the potatoes.

Traditionally, in my family, asparagus was served with either melted butter (preferably) or Hollandaise sauce (see recipe to the right.) The cooked ham was served on a separate plate. Everybody would take one slice at a time. We also serve new, peeled, boiled or steamed potatoes.

Note: It is good to reserve the asparagus broth for a delicious asparagus soup. If you don't want to prepare soup for this menu, freeze the broth in a container for another time.

Hollandaise sauce

Prepare sauce while the asparagus is simmering. You will need 3 cups of broth from the asparagus cooking pan.

Ingredients (serves 4):
6 Tbsp (60g) butter
1 Tbsp flour
1 Tbsp sugar
3 cups asparagus broth
2 egg yolks blended with 2 Tbsp cold water
Salt and white pepper to taste

Preparation:
Set aside 3 cups of asparagus broth. Melt butter in a separate saucepan, and slowly add flour, constantly stirring, to form a smooth cream. Then slowly add asparagus broth (constantly stirring) until it is a smooth, light, creamy sauce. Add sugar and bring to a boil, stir, and remove from heat.

In a separate cup blend egg yolks with 2 Tbsp cold water, add 2 Tbsp of the hot sauce, and carefully whisk until smooth. Add this to the sauce (off the stove) and keep whisking until a creamy consistency is achieved. Add salt and pepper to taste.

Important: don't boil this sauce any longer! As a friend said, the heat level here is of utmost importance or the sauce will curdle.

Note: I usually add a few grains of citric acid to give it a touch of lemon. The real gourmet cooks use fresh lemon juice, which makes the preparation an ordeal. So that's why this is lazy, but pretty safe, version.

Beverage: White Burgundy

Side Salad: Carrot salad with sweet and sour dressing

Ingredients (serves 4):
4 carrots, peeled
Juice of ½ medium size lemon
2 Tbsp almond oil or sunflower oil
1 tsp honey or sugar to taste
Sweet paprika, salt and white pepper to taste

Preparation:
Finely slice or grate the carrots into a deep bowl. Add lemon juice, oil, pepper, salt and honey or sugar. Dust with paprika and blend all ingredients.

I sometimes add a little ginger, but with asparagus, the taste should not be too fancy or it will distract from the delicate taste of the asparagus.

Dessert: Rhubarb-vanilla cream

Ingredients (serves 4):
2 lbs rhubarb, washed, peeled, diced
1 cup brown sugar
½ cup water
2 packages French vanilla pudding, Jello brand
1 cup whipping cream
2 Tbsp sugar
1 dash vanilla extract

Preparation:
In a saucepan, bring rhubarb, water and sugar to a boil, reduce heat, and simmer until rhubarb is soft. With a fork, shred pieces, then stir. Let cool.

Blend pudding powder into cold rhubarb sauce. Normally it shouldn't need any additional liquid. Refrigerate for about 1 hour.

Whip cream. Divide rhubarb pudding into 4 glass bowls and top with a cap of whipped cream.

Note: I recommend using French vanilla pudding because its vanilla aroma is the best. Also, you could add another teaspoon or to taste of vanilla extract if you wish. However, it should be the real vanilla extract.

In German markets, you can find vanilla sugar containing genuine vanilla, which is really good. You could also try to find a vanilla bean and add its contents to the rhubarb when you cook it.

Of course, you can use any other vanilla pudding, even if you would have to cook it. Then you could stir it into the hot rhubarb sauce as a replacement for the hot milk you normally would use. It's critical, though, that you have the right amount of liquid to achieve the right consistency.

Special dish of the month: Matjes (young herring fillets) with new potatoes in a creamy sauce

The first Matjes (young herring,) caught by fishermen each year in the Netherlands is reserved for the Queen of the Netherlands. Traditionally she is the one to open the Matjes season.

As the Rhineland is close to the Netherlands border, this delicacy is highly appreciated in this area. "Heringstipp," a dish made from Matjes pieces in a creamy sauce with apples and onions, has a special place in the May menus of families who eat fish.

Like the asparagus, Matjes is a seasonal dish. However, you can buy herring fillets out of season as well – they just aren't as good as the fresh ones. But don't let me discourage you from trying the off-season fillets as well. With this creamy sauce you get the best of this fish — promise.

The sauce is best when refrigerated overnight or at least for 3 hours to blend all the different flavors.

If you are confused because the recipe mentions "pairs" of fillets, the explanation is that they are gutted, but the tails are not cut off. The tails keep together the two sides of the fillets, which makes them a pair.

Traditionally this dish is served with a beer like "Dortmunder Export" (a Lager) or a crisp white wine like Chardonnay.

Ingredients (serves 4):
4 pairs of Matjes (young herring fillets)
1 medium onion, thinly sliced
1 tart apple (I like Braeburn)
1 Tbsp lemon juice, preferably freshly squeezed
1 medium size kosher pickle
5 Tbsp (100ml) white wine vinegar (actually I always use the vinegar in the pickle jar)
1 medium onion, peeled, finely diced
2 peppercorns
6 mustard seeds
2 bay leaves
1 cup (1/8 l) sour cream
1 cup (1/8 l) half & half
1 small bunch of dill or parsley, chopped

Preparation:
Peel apple, core and quarter, then thinly slice each quarter. Drizzle with lemon juice right away, so the apple slices keep their fresh color and don't discolor. Drain pickle, cut in half, seed and slice thinly.

In a saucepan, bring vinegar, peppercorns, mustard seeds, onions and bay leaves to a boil. Simmer for 5 minutes. Drain through a sieve or cheesecloth and pour juice back into the saucepan. Let cool, add half & half and sour cream, apples and sliced onions. Refrigerate for at least 2 hours, or overnight.

Before serving, place 1 pair of Matjes fillets on each dish. Ladle ¼ of the sauce on top and garnish with a dust of paprika powder for color. Serve with small peeled potatoes, steamed and sprinkled with chopped parsley or dill for garnish.

Note: This dish is often served with Schwarzbrot, the dark rye bread, spread with butter. Best beverage is a Pilsner or another light beer.

Time to get ready for the Rumtopf (fruit in Rum) that's to be enjoyed in December

What's a Rumtopf anyway? The fun part of this traditional fruit compote is that you have to work at it for about 6 months before you can actually enjoy it with vanilla pudding or vanilla ice cream.

Many of my friends back in Germany took exceptional pride in having the best Rumtopf recipe of all and served it in the cold winter time as a dessert. But, beware — it's very deceptive, and a no-no for children!

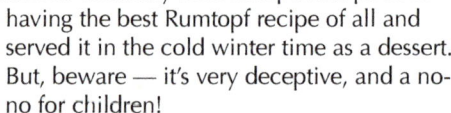

The Rumtopf (the pot used to make the compote) usually looks like the one in this picture and the pot itself also can be a piece of pride and a family treasure. As the fruit must not be exposed to sunlight during the time of "ripening," the pot is usually made of pottery.

Traditionally the Rumtopf was stocked with all fruits of the seasons for example blueberries or other berries could also be used,) and each month you'd add the seasonal fruit as it came freshly plucked or harvested. The harvest calendar on the previous page is for my part of the world, the U.S. Midwest so they may vary in other states.

In my experience, you get the best results following that old tradition. Follow the calendar to add that month's appropriate fruit to the pot so you can enjoy (not too much, though…) this nice tradition around Christmas time.

For more fruit, you need to adjust the amount of sugar accordingly.

Ingredients for one Rumtopf (about 1 gallon)
2 cups strawberries   + 2 cups sugar
1 cup sweet cherries pitted + ½ cup of sugar
1 cup pie cherries pitted + ½ cup of sugar
2 cups peaches, pitted, quartered + 1 cup of sugar
2 cups apricots, pitted, quartered + 1 cup of sugar
2 cups plums, pitted, halved + 1 cup of sugar
2 pears, peeled, cored and sliced + 1 cup of sugar
1 cup apples, peeled, cored and sliced + ½ cup of sugar
1 cup walnuts peeled
1 bottle of dark Rum (or more)

Preparation:
For the seasonal fruit, observe the calendar on the previous page and the amount of sugar according to the table above. Always wash fruit and pat dry, and don't peel, but pit or core where necessary.

Place fruit in Rumtopf, cover with the listed amount of sugar and drizzle with rum until fruits are covered. And each time you add fruit, cover the pot with a cheesecloth that is soaked in rum.

Start out with the first fruit of the year, strawberries, and sprinkle with the same amount of sugar. Next seasonal fruit would be cherries, sour and sweet; both kinds are needed. Place on top of strawberries and sprinkle with the ½ amount of sugar, and then drizzle with rum again, until fruits are covered.

Proceed with each fruit of the seasons, and make sure that rum covers all the fruit.

The Rumtopf is ready at the end of November.

It is traditionally served with vanilla pudding or vanilla ice cream. But be careful – too much of this at a time will make you regret it.

Did You Know? Asparagus ...

Germans expect the *Spargelzeit* (asparagus season, parallel with the *Erdbeerzeit* — strawberry season — from May to end of June) with a similar feverish anticipation Americans have for the NFL Playoffs in January. *Spargel*, German asparagus, is white, has to be peeled and is served with ham or pork, boiled potatoes and butter or hollandaise sauce. Green asparagus, the one we know over here in the USA, has been valued in Germany for only a short time.

Once, on a road trip, I listened to Garrison Keillor's Saturday morning radio show, and he reported from the Lanesboro's Rhubarb Festival in Minnesota. We have been to a Cherry Festival in Door County, Peach Festivals in British Columbia, Cherry Blossom Festivals in D.C. and Wine Festivals in California. Well, Germans have their *Spargel* Festivals, their yearly pilgrimages to their favorite asparagus farmers (some people keep this information as secret as Americans would keep their fishing spots,) and their yearly invitation to friends and family for a *Spargelessen* (asparagus dinner.) Cookbooks are dedicated to it, and every family has its own recipe for perfect asparagus. I like to compare this to our turkey stuffing recipes.

Asparagus has a long and interesting history.

The ancient Egyptians already appreciated this wild vegetable as food as well as for its medical properties. They called it "Divine Food," food reserved only for their pharaohs. Romans and Greeks first wrote about the agricultural cultivation of these stalks. And physicians like Hippocrates used its dried roots as a diuretic, but others also used it as an aphrodisiac. In Germany, asparagus was discovered in the 15th Century, used in cloister medicine, not as a vegetable. Only in the 16th Century, it was re-discovered as a vegetable, again as a delicacy for kings and princes all over Europe, too expensive for the "average" citizen. All of this was still green asparagus.

In the mid-1800s, farmers had covered the seedlings with covers of pottery against bugs and birds. The asparagus, deprived of sunlight, had a pale, not green, color, and — voila — white asparagus was born. Today, you can discover asparagus fields by their long rows of carefully heaped earth assuring asparagus stays white. It seems this variety quickly became the dominant one.

Eating asparagus came with pretty strict "do's and don'ts." Before the invention of stainless steel knives, white asparagus in Germany was eaten with fingers only and from the bottom to the top. It was considered bad manners to cut them with a knife, which used to be true for cutting potatoes as well. Now, it is good table manners to cut either one with knives and eat them using a fork. And being invited to a *Spargelessen* has to be treated as a special honor.

And if this is not enough information, the German city of Schrobenhausen proudly hosts the European Asparagus Museum (*Europäisches Spargelmuseum*.)

June in Köln

Main Portal of Kölner Dom, Cologne Cathedral

June in Köln

Who has not heard of Köln (Cologne,) the ancient city on the Rhine river?

The Kölner Dom (Cologne Cathedral,) built and rebuilt over a period of 500 years, is still constantly under repair. It is not only famous for its golden shrine of the three Magi (circa 1200,) but its Christmette (Christmas Midnight Service) is beautiful and well-known throughout the region. People come from other cities, driving for an hour or more, although they may have to stand in the cold church because there are not enough pews available. The lovely Old Town of Cologne has a charm of its own with many old restaurants and "Kneipen" (pubs,) where people stand at the bar and drink their "Kölsch." Kölsch is a light-colored beer indigenous to this city.

There is strong competition between Cologne and Düsseldorf concerning almost everything. Each city is trying to top anything the other city does, be it the tunnel along the Rhine river, the Karneval (mardi gras,) or the height of their TV towers. Cologne even added a tall radio antenna to its "Colonia" to make its tower 85 feet taller than its rival's "Rheinturm" (that's what the people of Düsseldorf say.) The citizens of Cologne have a reputation for being cunning people, and the city's most famous son, Konrad Adenauer, Germany's first chancellor after WWII, is one wonderful example of this. He and another city son, comedian Willy Millowitsch, were both famous for their adroitness and wittiness.

Cologne is one of the oldest of Germany's major cities. Its name goes back to the Romans, who named their city "Colonia Agrippina" in 50 A.D (after Agrippina, Emperor Claudius' wife.) It was Rome's imperial governor's residence, and quickly the city became one of the empire's most important trade and manufacturing centers north of the Alps. The Romans also brought Christianity to Cologne, and it quickly became a diocesan town. Charlemagne, in 785, founded the Archbishopric of Cologne.

During the Middle Ages, the city became the most populous and one of the wealthiest cities in the German-speaking world. In 1288, the citizens of Cologne defeated the bishop and ruler of their town and consequently took government and economic power into their hands. Around 1500, the city founded its first university. Cologne

Pictures from top right clockwise: Gürzenich Festival Hall, Botanical Garden, Cathedral, Hanse buildings, old cologne, Cathedral, Willi Millowitsch, Cologne's most famous comedian.

became a leading member of the "Hanse," the Hanseatic League, and a center of commercial fairs. With the discovery of the New World, however, things changed. New forms of business and trade routes were established; Europe transformed to national states, and Cologne's economic and political power declined. In 1794, Napoleon's troops occupied Cologne. In 1815, after Napoleon's defeat, it became part of the Kingdom of Prussia. As part of Prussia and later the German Kaiserreich, Cologne rose again. Now it is a business center and, due to its location, a transportation hub in Western Europe. It's also a university city, where young people make the city a more charming place, and its people are one of a kind – hearty, with a famous sense of humor.

The Cologne of today is a world-class city and tourist attraction. It is beloved for its fascinating blend of all that is good: past and present, history, art and culture, of ancient churches and old buildings, shopping, art galleries, , museums (like the Roman-Germanic and the East-Asian museums,) classical music, musical theater, and jazz festivals. People come together from all over to be part of the fun. You name it- Cologne has it – including the Cologne Cathedral, the most-visited building in Germany. The city is also an International center for commerce, trade fairs, auction houses like Sotheby's and exhibitions of all kinds.

There is an old Roman saying that "Anyone who has not seen Cologne has not seen Germany."

About the Menu

Cologne and the city of Düsseldorf, where I grew up, were rivals throughout history. The two cities have been competing for the rights to trade, as bishops' residences, as the capital of state, and until today, as being the best university city, having the highest TV tower, being the best tourist venue — you name it.

In culinary terms, however, there's not much difference between the traditional Cologne and Düsseldorf dishes, although nobody wants to admit that.

Goulash soup, pigs in a blanket, and the special dish of the month are very traditional recipes of this area.

In Cologne's Old Town, you will find quite a few wonderful, traditional restaurants where these dishes are being served. And, they are always paired with the house brew of beer, Koelsch.

Not surprisingly, the very same dishes are claimed to be the "local" specialty in both cities. And, during the months containing an "r" in their name (i.e. the months from October through April) you can enjoy "Muscheln Rheinische Art" (mussels, simmered in a broth of onions, carrots, and white wine.) Yummy!

June in Köln (Cologne)

Appetizer:
Celery root fried in lemon dressing with walnuts or pumpkin seeds

Soup:
Goulash soup

Entrée:
Pigs in a blanket with potatoes, carrots and gravy

Side salad:
Mushroom salad with garlic lemon vinaigrette

Dessert:
Chocolate cake à la Elisabeth

Beverage:
Beer, better a light brew than an ale type beer

Special dish of the month:
Himmel und Erde (Heaven and Earth) with either fried black pudding (traditionally) or fried chicken liver (for those who don't fancy black pudding)

And don't forget to add cherries to the Rumtopf

Appetizer: Celery root (celeriac,) fried, in a lemon dressing with walnuts or pumpkin seeds

Ingredients (serves 4):
4 celery roots (celeriac,) sliced in about ½" slices
4 Tbsp olive oil
1 tsp finely chopped parsley
1 Tbsp pumpkin seeds or walnuts
4 little bouquets of parsley

For the dressing:
1 Tbsp olive oil
1 Tbsp white vinegar
Pepper, salt to taste
1 Tbsp water
1 Tbsp lemon juice
1 tsp dry mustard

Preparation:
Heat 4 Tbsp oil in a cooking pan to medium heat, and fry celery root slices until they feel soft and are nicely brown on both sides. Set aside to cool. Mix rest of ingredients, except pumpkin seeds and parsley bouquets, for dressing and shake until smooth.

Place celery slices on 4 plates so they form a wheel. Top with vinaigrette. Sprinkle with pumpkin seeds and/or walnuts and garnish each plate with a parsley bouquet.

Note: If you want to refine this recipe, top the celery and vinaigrette with one tsp whipped cream mixed with a tsp of mustard and then top with pumpkin seeds and/or walnuts and parsley. But be careful — you add calories.

For vegetarian friends, I often serve a thick slice of fried celery root with a mushroom sauce (see July,) accompanied with grilled or steamed vegetables. In Germany, the celery root is known as "the meat of the vegetarian."

Soup: Goulash soup

Ingredients (serves 4):
2 lbs (ca. 1 kg) beef shoulder, washed and dried
2 lbs (ca. 1 kg) onions, peeled
1 tsp sage
1 bay leaf
Salt, pepper to taste
1 cup tomato paste
2 cups (½ l) red wine (or 2 cups beef broth + 1 tsp red vinegar)
2 cups (½ l) vegetable or beef broth
1 Tbsp vegetable oil

Preparation:
Dice meat into 1/2-inch pieces. Dice onions into the same size. In a saucepan heat oil to medium heat and sauté onions until transparent. Remove onions, increase heat and sear meat on all sides until brown. Stir in onions, then add tomato paste, and stir until meat and onions are covered. Add sage, bay leaf, pepper, salt, wine (or broth-vinegar mix,) and broth (beef or vegetable.) Bring to a boil, reduce heat, and simmer soup for about 2 hours.

Before serving, add salt and pepper to taste and, if desired, a dash of lemon juice or red wine vinegar.

Note: It's important that equal amounts of meat and onions are used.

One variation I like, although it wouldn't be the traditional recipe, i.e., to sauté two cloves of garlic with the onions. When I remove and set aside the onions, however, I discard the garlic before I sear the meat.

Entrée: Kohlrouladen (pigs in a blanket) with potatoes, carrots, and gravy

Ingredients (serves 4):
1 cabbage (set 8 big leaves aside, chop small leaves)
4 ground beef or pork patties
2 Tbsp vegetable oil
2 white onions, finely chopped
Pinch of marjoram
1 Tbsp mustard or to taste (at least 1 tsp)
Salt, pepper
2 Tbsp white wine
2 eggs
2 Tbsp bread crumbs or 1 roll soaked and squeezed dry
2 Tbsp vegetable oil
1 Tbsp flour
2 cups vegetable broth or white wine

Preparation:
In a saucepan, heat olive oil, and brown onions, chopped cabbage, and meat patties, stirring frequently. Remove from heat and drain. Grind or mix in a bowl, and add marjoram, mustard, pepper, salt, white wine, eggs, and roll or bread crumbs. Blend until it is a smooth paste, and set aside.

In a large saucepan, boil water and blanch the big cabbage leaves for about ½ minute. Dunk in cold water, drain and set aside to cool.

Place cabbage leaves on a large flat surface and spoon the meat paste on top. (It may seem odd that the paste is so relatively liquid, but that's the way it's supposed to be.)

Spoon at least 2 Tbsp paste on each cabbage leaf and fold the leaves over the meat mix. Fold the bottom end first, then the sides, and then the top, and fix the top with a toothpick.

If you have leftover cabbage/onion mix, cook it in a separate saucepan over medium heat in 1 Tbsp vegetable or olive oil, stirring frequently. Set aside and keep warm.

In a saucepan, heat 2 Tbsp vegetable oil to sizzling heat, and cook the cabbage wraps until nicely brown on all sides. Remove wraps from the saucepan and set aside.

Stir 1 Tbsp flour into remaining oil, then add vegetable broth or white wine, stirring frequently. Add a pinch of sugar, marjoram, and pepper and salt to taste. Serve as a sauce with pigs-in-a-blanket, steamed potatoes, and carrots, and the leftover sautéed cabbage/onion mix.

Note: You can substitute 4 Tbsp white egg substitute for the eggs, and 2 Tbsp Matzo meal for the roll or bread crumbs.

Beverage: Kölsch beer or a dry white wine like Pinot Grigio or Orvieto

Side salad: Mushroom salad with garlic lemon vinaigrette

Ingredients (serves 4):
2 cups (500g) fresh baby portobello mushrooms
2 spring onions, white and green parts
2 bunches fresh radishes
1 cup (125g) soy sprouts

For the dressing:
1 garlic clove mashed with ½ tsp salt
4 Tbsp freshly squeezed lemon juice
4 Tbsp olive oil
1 pinch of sugar
Salt, pepper to taste

For garnish:
1 bunch of watercress, washed, drained, and with stems snipped off.

Preparation:
Brush mushrooms and cut off stems, peel onions and slice crosswise. Wash radishes and cut in thin slices. Wash soy sprouts, drain, and pat dry and, mix vegetables together in a large bowl.

For the dressing, combine mashed garlic, lemon juice, and oil in a bowl and whisk until thick. Add sugar, salt and pepper to taste.

Drizzle dressing over salad, toss gently until salad is coated, and let sit for about 10 minutes.

Serve salad on individual salad plates, garnished with watercress.

Dessert: Chocolate cake à la Elisabeth

Ingredients (serves 4):
14 Tbsp (ca. 200g) butter, softened
1 cup (250g) sugar
6 eggs, whites and yolks separated
1 cup (250 g) ground almonds
7 ounce (200 g) bittersweet chocolate, cut into small pieces
½ cup (125 g) flour
1 tsp baking powder
1 pinch salt
grated zest from ½ lemon
1 tsp cinnamon
½ cup cornflakes, crumbled

Preparation:
Preheat oven to 375°F (190°C)

Mix flour and baking powder. Beat butter, sugar, and egg yolks until foaming. Stir in salt, lemon zest, and cinnamon, and slowly add the flour mixture. Beat egg whites until peaks are firm, and fold egg whites into cake mixture. Then fold in chocolate pieces and ground almonds.

Grease 9" springform pan and drizzle with crumbled corn¬flakes. Pour in the cake mixture and bake at 375°F for 1 hour or until a toothpick, inserted in center comes out clean.

Note: In Germany, cakes are traditionally served with whipped cream, but this cake also tastes delicious served with vanilla ice cream.

June in Köln

Special dish of the month: Himmel und Erde (Heaven and Earth) with chicken liver or fried black pudding

One of my favorites, this traditional specialty is very well-liked, and best known in the Rhineland area around Cologne and Düsseldorf. Black pudding is a sausage made from the blood of pigs. It is very common in Germany, in the U.S., I only found it in specialty shops or on the Internet.

I grew up with it, and every time we go to Cologne, or one of the old traditional restaurants in Düsseldorf, I have to have it.

Some restaurants serve it with mashed potatoes. The cooked apples, thickly sliced, are also served on the side. The black pudding may be arranged around or on top of the potatoes, and then, on top of that pyramid, the dish is garnished with crisp onion rings. Other restaurants serve the mashed potatoes in the middle of the plate, with apples and black pudding arranged around it, and crisply fried onion rings as the garnish on top. There are as many arts of serving as there are restaurants, so wherever you go, there may be a different way of presentation.

So here's the 999th way (my family's variation) of preparing my favorite dish. What does not change, though, are the three major ingredients: potatoes for Earth/Erde, apples for Heaven/Himmel, and black pudding.

And heartily sautéed chicken livers came into vogue fairly recently, created by a fashionable new chef who wanted to do something different. They do taste very good, too.

The beverage for this feast should be a Kölsch beer, but a Lager beer should do as well. Beer, is a must with this hearty dish, even for wine lovers like me.

In Cologne, Kölsch is served in these long, slim glasses. In Düsseldorf's Old Town, the Altstadt, you will find the local brew, the "Altbier," a dark, sometimes more bitter beer served in short, stout glasses.

Needless to say, that here, too, there is a strong patriotic feeling about which beer is the best. A "real" Düsseldorfer will never even consider agreeing that Kölsch has its merits. But, as everywhere, tourists don't care, and today you can find many Kneipen serving Kölsch in Düsseldorf as well. Finding Altbier in Cologne—now that is a different story.

Ingredients (serves 4):
2½ lbs (ca. 700 g) potatoes
2 lbs (900 g) apples (I prefer Braeburn)
2/3 cup (150 g) finely diced bacon
½ cup finely diced onions
1 pinch of salt and sugar
4 Tbsp butter
1 lb (450 g) black pudding
1 dash white wine vinegar to taste

Preparation:
Peel potatoes, steam until tender, mash immediately, and set aside. In the meantime, peel and core apples, dice, and simmer with 2 Tbsp water until tender, and cook onions and bacon in a saucepan, until onions are golden and a little crisp.

Combine potatoes and apples and add salt and sugar to taste.

Cut black pudding into 16 thick slices (or enough thick slices to divide into 4 servings) and dust lightly with flour. Heat 4 Tbsp butter to medium, and sauté black pudding slices until crisp on both sides.

On 4 dinner plates, place potato/apple mixture in middle, garnish with slices of black pudding, and top with golden onion/bacon mix. Enjoy.

Note: "Googling" has some magic. I found out, that the Irish and British cuisine regards black pudding as a delicacy, as many descendants of Irish provenance probably know.

If you cannot find black pudding or are not a fan of it, you could substitute chicken liver, sautéed with onions and bacon. And if you'd like to find out more about black pudding, look under Cologne references.

July in Frankfurt

The Römer, Frankfurt's Historic Center

July in Frankfurt

"Frankfurt-Rhine-Main" is the largest airport in Germany, Frankfurt is the financial center of the European Union, and Frankfurt is in the center of Germany's chemical industry. Today's Frankfurt is one of the most important economic centers in Germany—a bustling modern industrial center. Its high-rise buildings have earned it the nickname "Mainhattan" (Manhattan on the Main river.)

In addition to its cosmopolitan charm, however, this old town is also a historic and cultural center is well worth visiting.

Frankfurt's cultural life is famous for its diversity. In the city and on the Museumsufer, "the museum embankment" along the Main river, one finds more than 100 art galleries and renowned museums with exhibitions from historic to contemporary art. The music scene offers internationally recognized artists, and musical events are everywhere.

There are small parks at every corner. Frankfurt's famous Palmengarten has 45,000 square feet of greenhouses, a world-famous collection of tropical plants, outdoor concerts during the summer, a wonderful indoor restaurant, and much more.

On warm summer evenings, the city's taverns with their beer gardens and patios attract everybody to sit outside. We loved to sit on a patio along the banks of the Main river, enjoy a drink or "Ebbelwoi" (apple wine, served in a "Bembel" the typical gray and blue jug.) Students at the city's large university also add to the young and buzzing atmosphere of the city.

History has also left its mark on Frankfurt throughout the centuries. Although unimportant in Roman times, it became an influential town under Charlemagne. Granted "city rights" in 1254, Frankfurt became increasingly independent and, from 1372 on, reported only and directly to the German Kaiser, the emperor. Later, until the 18th century, German kings were elected in Frankfurt. And then, in 1815, after the defeat of Napoleon, Frankfurt became a free city. It joined the German Confederation together with 35 German states and other free cities.

Pictures from top right clockwise: Frankfurt Financial Center ("Mainhattan,") Sachsenhausen, the "Kneipen Neighborhoodd," old Frankfurt, Museumsufer, Paulskirche, Rheingau, Frankfurt's surrounding area, Palmengarten, area map

In 1848, the Frankfurt National Assembly, for the first time freely elected by the German people, made an attempt to unify Germany and to guarantee civil rights. They failed, and 23 years later Prussion chancellor Otto von Bismarck finally succeeded in doing so. The Paulskirche, where the assembly convened, is an interesting museum depicting this time in history.

Next to it stands the Römer, Frankfurt's beautifully restored 15th-century city hall; Frankfurt established its world-famous Book Fair in 1480, and the Frankfurt Auto Show attracts visitors from all over the world.

The surrounding region boasts beautiful vineyards, recreational parks, nature preserves and the hills of Taunus, just 30 minutes outside the city. I love visiting the old-fashioned spa towns (towns where people go to regain or sustain their health; usually these towns are famous for their waters or healthy air) like Idstein, with hiking trails and countless other activities nearby, including river rafting and mountain biking.

The scenic Rheingau wine region is a "must" for wine lovers. And there is much more to see than just wine, good food and Frankfurt's famous Green Sauce (a sauce made of herbs, available at all farmers' markets,) served with meat and potatoes.

About the Menu

Somebody once told me that vegetarian cooking is truly boring, but I don't believe that's true.

Friends in Germany, who are vegetarians, showed me how to cook without meat and satisfy even a meat lover like my husband, Chuck. So here are his favorites, and none of them are boring. In our house, we have a vegetarian delight at least one day per week, so I offer three choices of salads you can interchange.

The mixed bell pepper salad is easily prepared in the microwave. The vegetable soup is best prepared fresh from scratch and doesn't take much time, and you can prepare the egg dumplings for the soup ahead of time. I especially love the Mushroom Schnitzel. And if you think it's not enough, serve a side of steamed, peeled potatoes.

In Germany, this menu goes with a nice, cool beer, I prefer wine (and for this menu a red, rather than white.) If you wanted to pair this menu with beer, I'd recommend a dark beer.

And, the sauerkraut quiche surely is a pretty "off the beaten path" dish, but it's delicious, and you'll love the combination of sauerkraut, nuts, cream and cheese.

July in Frankfurt am Main

Appetizer:
Mixed bell pepper salad with Italian dressing

Soup:
Vegetable soup with egg dumplings

Entrée:
Mushroom Schnitzel with creamy sauce and green beans

Side salads:
Tomato salad with red onions in vinaigrette
Spinach salad with mustard dressing

Dessert:
Kirschmichel (Cherry Crumble)

Beverage:
Red Zinfandel

Special dish of the month:
Sauerkraut quiche

Time to add Peaches to the Rumtopf!

Appetizer: Mixed bell pepper salad with Italian dressing

Ingredients (serves 4):
1 red bell pepper
1 yellow bell pepper
1 orange bell pepper (or another red bell pepper)
1 green bell pepper

For the marinade/dressing:
3 Tbsp extra virgin olive oil
2 Tbsp balsamic vinegar (or red wine vinegar)
1 tsp lemon juice
1 Tbsp water
Pepper, salt to taste
2 Tbsp Italian herbs
4 sprigs of basil for garnish
4 black olives, whole or sliced, for garnish
4 tsp grated parmesan, optional

Preparation:
Seed the bell peppers and julienne. When I have the time, I skin them before cutting (see note below) because the peppers taste so much better then.

Mix marinade/dressing. Place the bell peppers in a large saucepan, pour marinade/dressing over them, and cook over medium heat until the bell peppers are al dente, and the marinade/dressing has a creamy consistency.

Remove from heat, stir, and let cool. On 4 plates, distribute the salad and garnish with a sprig of basil, olives, and parmesan.

Note: To skin peppers, place them in the oven at high heat and bake until the skin has blisters. Cool for a moment, and remove the skin, which should come off easily

Soup: Vegetable soup with egg dumplings

Ingredients (serves 4):
1 shallot
2 Tbsp vegetable oil (I prefer olive oil)
2 carrots
¼ piece celery root (celeriac)
1 parsley root (available in co-op stores)
4 small potatoes
1 cup of green beans
6 cups of vegetable broth (Use natural or organic broth if possible. It contains less salt and has a better flavor)
White pepper and salt, to taste
1 pinch sugar
½ bunch chopped parsley
2 leaves of Savoy cabbage (optional,) deveined
1 tsp dried garden herbs, like thyme, tarragon, and marjoram

Preparation:
Peel carrots, celery root, shallots, parsley root, and potatoes, and cut into about 1" pieces. In a large saucepan, heat vegetable oil and cook shallots in oil until they start to turn transparent. Add vegetable broth, and sugar, salt, and pepper to taste. Add garden herbs and bring to a boil. Simmer for 10 minutes, then add carrots, green beans, and potatoes. Simmer until carrots are al dente.

Cut the Savoy cabbage leaves in half and then into 1"-wide strips. Add to simmering soup, stir, and remove soup from heat immediately. Ladle soup into 4 bowls and garnish with chopped parsley. Serve with French bread, if desired.

Note: If you and/or your guests don't like the taste of cooked celery root, you can use it whole for cooking, and then remove it before serving the soup. However, it's essential to simmer it with the broth, because it gives the soup a wonderful taste.

Egg dumplings

Ingredients (serves 4):
4 eggs
2 Tbsp heavy whipping cream
¼ tsp salt
1 pinch nutmeg

Preparation:
Mix all ingredients in a blender until smooth. In a large saucepan, bring 1 quart of water to a boil, and put a steamer into the saucepan. Put a sheet of aluminum foil in a square container (plastic, steel or porcelain,) so that the foil overlaps the container. Pour the egg mixture into the container, place it in the steamer, and, without stirring, let the mixture become firm over boiling water. Remove from the pot and let cool. Lift edges of aluminum foil and turn egg mixture onto a plate. With a wet knife, cut into cubes. Serve with clear soups or in a salad.

Note: You can pep up these dumplings by adding fresh or dried herbs like chives, parsley or Italian herb mix, depending on what kind of flavor you want to give your soup.

To present these egg dumplings in a more fancy way, try this: prepare as described above, with or without added herbs or spices, and then use cookie cutters to cut the dumplings into different shapes.

I use this as an addition to salads sometimes, and it's always good, especially with spinach salad and mustard sauce.

Here are two more kinds of dumplings for soups that are favorites in German kitchens. They can be prepared easily ahead of time and then frozen and used as needed. Use 4 bowls of vegetable or chicken soup for these recipes.

Parsley dumplings

Ingredients (serves 4):
2 eggs, beaten
1 Tbsp chopped parsley
1 Tbsp butter softened
Salt and pepper to taste
½ cup flour or corn meal

Preparation:
Bring vegetable broth to a boil and reduce heat to a simmer.
Mix all ingredients together, Form small dumplings, add to broth, and simmer for about 5 minutes, or until done.

Marrow dumplings

Ingredients (serves 4):
1 marrow bone (available from any good butcher)
1 cup bread cubes, soaked and drained (press firmly)
1 egg, beaten
Salt, pepper and nutmeg to taste

Preparation:
Scratch marrow out of bone and melt in a saucepan over medium heat. Remove from heat. Add other ingredients, mix well and form small dumplings. Add to boiling broth or soup, reduce heat and simmer for 10 minutes.

Entrée: Mushroom Schnitzel with green beans in creamy mushroom sauce

Ingredients (serves 4):
1 lb fresh chanterelle mushrooms
2 finely diced white onions
1 cup finely chopped fresh parsley
2 Tbsp butter
2 dinner rolls, 2 days old, without crust, soaked in water and squeezed dry
1 additional Tbsp bread crumbs, or more (if needed)
1 steamed, cooled potato
1 egg, slightly beaten
½ tsp anchovy paste
1 dash soy sauce
black pepper, salt to taste

For the coating:
4 Tbsp flour
2 eggs
1 cup of bread crumbs

For garnish:
4 lemon slices
4 sprigs of parsley for garnish
4 portions of steamed green beans
3 Tbsp butter and 1 Tbsp vegetable oil for frying
For the sauce:
2 cups vegetable broth
1 tsp mustard, optional
½ cup whipping cream or sour cream, optional

Preparation:
Clean mushrooms, trim and quarter. In a saucepan, heat 1 Tbsp butter to medium heat, and sauté mushrooms, onions and parsley, until mushrooms start to fry.

Add the two dinner rolls, mash using a fork, and sauté with mushroom mix. Remove from heat, and mix with a fork or in a blender, until smooth. Or, if you have a meat grinder, that would be the best tool to use. When everything is well blended, add the potato and blend again.

Let cool, and then fold in 1 egg. If the mixture is too liquid, add 1 Tbsp of bread crumbs, or enough to make the mixture formable. Season with anchovy paste, soy sauce, and salt and pepper to taste.

Have 3 deep dishes ready, one each for flour, 2 beaten eggs, and breadcrumbs. Form flat, 3" round (burger-sized) schnitzels, and coat first in flour, then in egg mixture, and last in bread crumbs. In a frying pan, heat 3 Tbsp butter and 1 Tbsp vegetable oil to medium heat, and fry schnitzels on both sides until golden brown. Remove from pan, increase heat and add 2 cups vegetable broth to liquid to the pan, Bring to a boil, stirring frequently. Salt and pepper to taste. If you wish to have a creamy sauce, add 1 tsp mustard and ½ cup whipping cream or sour cream.

Using 4 dinner plates, ladle sauce on first, then place schnitzel on top. Garnish each plate with a slice of lemon and a bouquet of parsley. Serve with steamed green beans.

Note: Sometimes it's hard to find chanterelle mushrooms. Although they are best for this recipe, you can use criminis or Portobello mushrooms instead. Also, shiitake mushrooms are wonderful, especially when served with steamed green asparagus. Another story is the gusto of Germans for fresh (and personally gathered) mushrooms, but that story is told in October!

Beverage: Red Zinfandel or Roter Spätburgunder (Red Burgundy) from Germany

Side salads: Tomato salad with red onion vinaigrette or Spinach salad with mustard dressing

Tomato salad with red onion vinaigrette

Ingredients (serves 4):
2 large tomatoes or 1 can diced tomatoes, drained

For the dressing:
1 clove garlic
½ finely chopped red onion
5 Tbsp extra virgin olive oil
4 Tbsp red Balsamic vinegar
½ red onion, finely sliced, almost shaved
Pepper, salt to taste
4 Tbsp finely chopped parsley

Preparation:
Skin tomatoes (if you want to be fancy) by dunking them quickly into boiling water, which makes it easy to remove the skin. Then remove seeds and white parts, and cut tomatoes into 1" large pieces.

Peel garlic and cut into two pieces. Rub the inside of a large bowl with the cut side of the garlic, which gives a fine aroma, but not the taste of garlic, to the salad. Mix olive oil and vinegar, chopped onions, pepper and salt in this bowl, add tomatoes, and toss gently.

Divide onto 4 salad plates, top with onion slices, and drizzle on top the leftover vinaigrette from the bowl. Garnish with chopped parsley.

Alternative: Spinach salad with mustard dressing

Ingredients (serves 4):
1 lb fresh spinach, washed, and stemmed
1 cup bacon, fried crisp, drained, crumbled (see Note)
¼ lb mushrooms sliced (optional)
1 cup sliced water chestnuts or 1 small red onion, chopped
1 cup sliced radishes (optional)
1 cup diced black olives (optional)
2 hard boiled eggs, egg yolks mashed with a fork and set aside, egg whites diced

For the dressing:
2 egg yolks, mashed
½ tsp salt
1½ tsp sugar
1 Tbsp coarsely ground black pepper
1 clove crushed garlic
1 Tbsp water
1 Tbsp Dijon mustard
5 Tbsp heavy cream
½ tsp horseradish
¼ cup red wine vinegar or white balsamic vinegar

Preparation:
Blend dressing ingredients. In a large bowl, combine ingredients (except egg whites) for salad. Drizzle salad with dressing, tossing gently until all is coated. Divide onto 4 salad plates and sprinkle with egg whites.

Note: To make the dressing lighter you can substitute 2 Tbsp yogurt and 4 Tbsp sour cream for the heavy cream.

For vegetarians: Now there are non-meat bacon "bits" available in Co-op and other markets, so you don't have to miss out on its wonderful flavor.

Dessert: Kirschmichel (Cherry Crumble)

Cherries are one of the most beloved summer fruits in Germany, and this cherry dish is found throughout Germany's kitchens.

My mother told me "Take a handful of this, and a spoonful of that. Don't forget the sugar, and beat the egg white very firm. And don't overheat, and make sure that you pit all the cherries, oh, and … "

So I needed to find a recipe that would work over here as well. In checking all my cookbooks and the Internet, I ran across dozens of recipes that sometimes varied considerably.

This one is the version that most resembles this beloved dessert with which I grew up. I found it on the Internet at http://www.kochen-und-schlemmen.de and translated it. It is the Hessian version of the recipe. As Germany has as many, if not more, dialects as it has states, this dessert has a different name in the Frankfurt (state of Hessen) area; it's called Kerscheplotzer (KAR-shey-PLOT-tsar).

Ingredients (serves 4):
8 dinner rolls, 2 days old, without crust, thinly sliced
2 cups (500 ml) 2% milk
4 Tbsp (50 g) butter
1/3 cup (75g) sugar

4 eggs, divided
1 grated lemon zest
2 lbs (900 g) sweet cherries, pitted
2 Tbsp butter to grease the 9"-deep baking pan
4 Tbsp butter
1 Tbsp cinnamon, mixed with 1 tsp sugar

Preparation:
Preheat oven to 400°F (200°C)

Heat milk to lukewarm temperature, place in a flat dish, and put the thinly sliced dinner rolls into the milk. Whisk butter with sugar, egg yolks and lemon zest until foamy. Add dinner roll/milk mixture and blend. Stir in cherries. Beat egg whites until peaks are firm, and carefully fold into cherry mixture.

Grease the 9"-deep baking pan and add cherry mixture.

Cut 4 Tbsp butter into thin pieces, and sprinkle on top. Then sprinkle on cinnamon-sugar mixture. Bake for 45 minutes at 400°F.

Note: Serve hot from baking dish, maybe with a side of vanilla ice cream or topped with whipped cream.

Special dish of the month: Sauerkraut Quiche

When vegetarian friends first served this dish to me and my meat-loving husband, I was sure he would turn up his nose (not visibly, of course, that wouldn't have been polite.) It most certainly it would never become part of our menu plan. But he loved it! Ever since, this has been one of our favorite vegetarian dishes.

Ingredients (serves 4):

Pastry for quiche:
1 cup flour
4 Tbsp butter softened
1 tsp baking powder
2 Tbsp milk

For the filling:
1 Tbsp butter
3 Tbsp bread crumbs
1 onion
¾ to 1 cup crumbled bacon or diced ham
1 can of sauerkraut, drained, and chopped
⅓ cup (50g) ground hazelnuts
¾ cup (200g) sour cream
3 Tbsp milk 2%
1 egg, beaten

Salt, pepper to taste
1 cup (100g) grated young Gouda or mild Cheddar or Emmental cheese

Preparation:
Preheat oven to 525°F (275°C)

Blend butter, flour and baking powder in a large mixing bowl. Add milk and blend carefully. I never use a blender, because this pastry is much better just stirred with a wooden spoon. Form a ball, cover and set aside for 20 minutes.

In a saucepan, heat 1 Tbsp butter and sauté onions (and bacon or ham if desired,) stir in hazelnuts and sauerkraut, and sauté for 2 minutes, then set aside.

Mix sour cream with egg, milk, salt, and pepper to taste. Blend half of this mixture with the sauerkraut mix, and set the other half aside.

Place pastry in a baking dish and spread evenly to line the bottom and part of the sides. Sprinkle on half of the grated cheese. Pour sauerkraut mixture over cheese, spreading it evenly. Top with rest of sour cream mixture. Mix the breadcrumbs into the other half of the grated cheese and sprinkle on top of baking dish.

Bake for 20 minutes at 525°F, then reduce heat to 350°F (175°C,) and bake for another 10 minutes, or until a toothpick comes out clean. Serve in the dish along with a green salad with a creamy dressing.

Goes well with beer or white wine.

Note: If you are allergic to wheat or grain products, use dried mashed potatoes instead of the breadcrumbs.

For vegetarians: use non-meat bacon or leave it out

Did You Know? Sauerkraut ...

Who has not heard of the Krauts? The British during WWI and the Americans in WWII called their German enemies by this name. An, of course, Sauerkraut is a favorite in European (not only German) cuisine. The Germans call it Sauerkraut, the French Choucroute, the peoples of Belarus, Ukraine, Russian, Poland, Czech, Bulgaria, Romania, and most Eastern European and Asian countries, they all have their own names for it. Mostly paired with pork, Germans add Juniper berries, and recipes in Alsace-Lorraine call for white wine or champagne. It is served with sausages of all kinds, bacon, ham, blood sausage, with potatoes or noodles, depending on the region throughout the world.

Sauerkraut with pork is a traditional New Year's Eve dish in Dutch Pennsylvania, thought to bring good luck for the upcoming year. And don't we all know it as a condiment on hot dogs?

Sauerkraut is only one of many varieties of fermented food worldwide, think of Kimchi in Korea, or fermented cabbage in Chinese cooking. According to reports, Chinese workers, who built the Great Wall about 2,000 years ago, lived mainly on fermented cabbage. According to legend, Genghis Khan introduced it to Europe during his invasion about 1,000 years ago. Plini wrote about fermented cabbage in ancient Rome about 2,000 years ago.

The South American variety is called Cortido, prepared with onions, cloves and oregano. In Africa cabbage is not popular and I have not found a fermented cabbage recipe. In Australia and New Zealand, sauerkraut is quite popular and has been due to the influence of the sailors under Captain Cook.

I have learned there is a significant difference between fresh sauerkraut and its canned cousins. Sauerkraut is high in Vitamin C, B and K. Fresh sauerkraut still contains all the bacteria good for our intestines.

Howeveer, canned and jarred kraut, depending on its treatment for preservation, probably does not. It is important to rinse fresh sauerkraut before using it in any way, due to its very high salt content.

American physicians used it during the Civil War to keep their POWs alive, and millions of people drink its juice to prevent diseases. Dutch sailors used it during their long sea travels to prevent scurvy, and Captain Cook used to haul along large amounts of it for the same reason, and because it could be kept over a long period of time.

And here is a fun little story: During World War I, the American food industry re-labeled it "liberty cabbage" as they feared the public would reject food with a German name.

Do you want more information? The Sauerkraut Museum in Stottsville, Penssylvanie will happily tell you all you would ever want (or not want) to know.

August on the Mosel River

Wine Fest at Cochem Castle and its Old Town

August on the Mosel River

Wine and tourism are the defining industries in the Mosel-Saar-Ruwer region, which is especially fascinating during harvest time. Most wine growers cannot use harvesting machines because the hills are too steep, so Germans from all areas make yearly pilgrimages to this and other wine areas to help with the harvesting. Their reward: to taste the wines for free. Others come to taste the new fresh wines (Federweisser) and buy the wines of the previous years. The "Federweisser" (Feather White) is a wonderful wine, traditionally served with a side of onion pie, but be careful! It tastes like lemonade, has the alcohol content of a normal wine, but still contains most of the sugar that would dissolve after the time of fermentation. You drink too much, and the hangover of the next morning is spectacular and makes you wish you had never heard of this treat.

The area from Koblenz to Trier seems to consist of endless vineyards, all boasting large signs showing their brand names — world-famous names like "Piesporter Goldtropfen," "Trittenheimer Altärchen" and many others.

The headwaters of the Mosel river are in France, in the beautiful Vosges mountains, where the river is called the "Moselle." It is 340 miles long and flows from France through Luxembourg and Germany into the Rhine river at "Deutsches Eck" (German Corner) by Koblenz. Because the Mosel flows through the industrial areas of Lorraine, France was adamant about having to "tame" the river. So today, the Mosel is mostly canalized, with 18 locks and dams, and is an important shipping route from France to the Rhine. In summer, there are as many cruise ships and sight-seeing boats on the river as there are cargo ships.

Pictures from top right clockwise: Foggy sunrise in Cochem, Trier Porta Nigra, Cochem Castle, wine harvest, Beilstein vineyards, Mosel town, Traben Trabach, Deutsches Eck Koblenz, Saarburg, area and river maps

Trier, in France called by its old name "Treves," is supposedly the oldest town in Germany. The city was first settled by the "Treveri", a Gaulic tribe.

Caesar Augustus founded the Roman town about 16 B.C. and called it "Augusta Treverorum." Trier contains some ancient Roman structures, including a bridge across the Mosel, built about the 2nd century, the ruins of an old Roman thermal spa, and the Porta Nigra (black gate.) Trier's Catholic cathedral holds the relic of Christ's robe, for which the Roman soldiers "cast lots."

The castle in Cochem still shows the glamor of its previous owners. It is not the only castle in this area, but it is a popular tourist attraction open to the public, as is the Wine Museum in Traben-Trarbach.

A tour along the river gives you many opportunities to enjoy a wonderful landscape, picturesque little villages hiding away from the main roads, good food and, yes, wonderful Riesling and other white wines.

About the Menu

One of my favorite salad ingredients is Belgian endive, a very common vegetable in Germany. I like it because of its fresh and sweet taste. To enjoy this vegetable, though, one must remove the bitter part on the bottom of the bulb. I also like just to steam Belgian endive and serve it with a tomato sauce as a light entrée or appetizer, served with warm, crusty French bread and white wine.

As for the soup, a clear chicken bouillon is not only delicious but also (and don't we all know that!) a great "medicine" for people who are sick. And on a cold winter day it revives the soul and warms the body.

Sole is one of Europe's finest fish, and this recipe with kohlrabi, another very delicate vegetable, in a carrot sauce, is a wonderful combination.

The peach mousse is best made with fresh peaches, but canned peaches, carefully drained, will do as well.

We can get a good Riesling wine or wine from the Mosel River (or the Mosel-Saar-Ruwer area in Germany,) in almost any good liquor or wine store in the U.S., but if Riesling is not available, try a Sauvignon Blanc or a Gewurztraminer.

August on the Mosel River

Appetizer:
Belgian endive with mandarin oranges in sour cream dressing

Soup:
Chicken bouillon with dumplings

Entrée:
Sole in carrot cream with risotto and kohlrabi

Side salad:
Cucumber salad in dill dressing

Dessert:
Peach mousse

Beverage:
Riesling or another white wine from the Mosel area

Special dish of the month:
Mini meatloaves in creamy mushroom sauce on crispy potatoes

Now is the time to add apricots to the Rumtopf

Appetizer: Belgian endive with mandarin oranges in sour cream dressing

In Germany, Belgian endive is known as "Chicorée" lettuce, whereas "Endivien" lettuce in Germany is the name for our American curly endive lettuce.

Belgian endive needs to be cored carefully, removing the bitter parts at the bottom of the vegetable. Cut a triangle from the bottom and try a piece of the core to see whether there are still some bitter parts left before using the rest of the bulb.

Ingredients (serves 4):
4 bulbs Belgian endive
2 8 ounce cans of mandarin oranges
4 Tbsp sour cream
2 tsp juice from mandarin oranges
Salt and white pepper to taste
4 mint leaves for garnish

Preparation:
Remove bitter parts from Belgian endive bulbs, and cut rest of bulbs crosswise into large 1" strips. Drain mandarin oranges very carefully, preserving the juice in a separate container.

In a large bowl, mix 4 Tbsp sour cream with 2 tsp mandarin orange juice. Add pepper and salt to taste. If consistency is not juicy enough, add another few drops of juice, and blend well. Add Belgian endive leaves and toss carefully. Add mandarin oranges, keeping 4 Tbsp for garnish.

Toss and distribute on 4 salad plates. Garnish with remaining mandarin oranges. Top each plate with one mint leaf to add a third color to the picture.

Soup: Chicken bouillon with semolina dumplings

Ingredients (serves 4):
1 stewing chicken (about 2 lbs)
1 yellow onion (do NOT peel)
1 bay leaf
1 Tbsp black peppercorns
½ tsp salt
¼ celery root (celeriac)
1 carrot
1 small leek
½ parsley root or 2 sprigs parsley

Preparation:
Cut chicken into 4 pieces. Peel carrot and celery root, clean leek, and cut all into fairly large pieces as they are going to be discarded later on. Put chicken and vegetables in a tall saucepan, and add enough water to cover chicken. Add peppercorns, bay leaf and salt. Bring to a boil, cover, reduce heat, and simmer for about 1 hour.

Remove chicken and pour bouillon through a sieve covered with cheesecloth. If the bouillon is not quite clear, beat two egg whites very stiff, return bouillon to the stove and bring to a simmer again. Carefully stir in stiff egg whites. They will "collect" all the little leftover ingredients. Remove egg whites with a slotted spoon or pour through the sieve again. The bouillon should be clear now. Ladle into 4 soup bowls, add semolina dumplings (recipe see next page,) and sprinkle with chopped parsley.

Note: If you add the unpeeled onion to the chicken, the onion peel will add a warm, golden color to the bouillon.

Not enough time to go through this whole procedure? You can buy good canned chicken broth in gourmet markets these days – but be sure to buy a brand that does not have too much sodium and salt.

Semolina dumplings

Ingredients (serves 4):
2 Tbsp butter
1 egg
salt
3 ounces semolina
1 tsp cold water

Preparation:
Melt and whisk the butter. Stir in the other ingredients one at a time. Allow to stand for 20 minutes. If too stiff, add a little water; if not stiff enough, add a little semolina and let sit for another 20 minutes. Scoop out dumplings with a teaspoon, drop gently into simmering, salted water and simmer until dumplings rise to the surface. Remove with a slotted spoon and serve in hot broth.

Entrée: Sole with carrot cream on risotto and kohlrabi

Ingredients:
4 sole fillets
2 carrots
1 Tbsp olive oil
8 Tbsp heavy cream
Salt and white pepper to taste
1 cup (¼ l) white wine like Chardonnay
1 dash lemon juice, optional

Preparation:
Peel and finely dice carrots. Saute in olive oil until tender. Add white wine, stir, and reduce heat to simmer. Add sole fillets and simmer (don't boil!) for about 10 minutes, or until fish is flaky. Remove fish from pan and keep warm. To make the sauce, add cream and salt and pepper to pan. The sauce needs a soft, tangy taste, so if it's not tangy enough, add a dash of white wine or lemon juice.

Cook sauce, stirring, until creamy. Blend in a food processor, Garnish with finely chopped parsley, and serve with kohlrabi and risotto,

Side Dish: Kohlrabi

Ingredients (serves 4):
4 kohlrabi

Preparation:
Peel kohlrabi and cut 1"long and ½" thick. Steam over salted water until tender. Add salt and white pepper to taste and 1 tsp butter and toss gently.

Side Dish: Risotto

Ingredients (serves 4):
2 cups Arborio rice (short grain, Italian rice)
4 cups water
1 Tbsp salt
½ carrot, peeled and finely diced
½ cup small frozen green peas, thawed
¼ white onion, finely chopped
1 Tbsp vegetable oil, preferably sunflower oil

Preparation:
In a large saucepan, heat oil and sauté carrot and onion until onion is transparent. Add rice and stir until rice is coated with oil. Slowly add water, stirring frequently. Add salt and pepper. Bring to a boil, Reduce heat to a simmer, stir in peas. Place a kitchen towel on top of the pan, and cover with lid, to close the pot tightly. Simmer for about 40 minutes, or until the liquid is completely absorbed. Fluff with a fork and let sit for another 5 minutes before serving.

Note: Arborio rice is available in all supermarkets these days

Beverage: Riesling or light beer

Side salad: Cucumber salad with dill dressing

Ingredients (serves 4):
1 English cucumber
½ tsp salt
½ white onion
2 Tbsp lemon juice
1 Tbsp water
5 Tbsp grapeseed oil
1 Tbsp dill weed
1 pinch salt, or to taste
1 pinch white pepper, or to taste
Paprika, for garnish
4 sprigs fresh dill or 4 dill blossoms for garnish
1 more dash of lemon juice, if needed

Preparation:
Wash cucumber and slice very thin. Sprinkle with ½ tsp salt, toss gently and set aside for 10 minutes. Drain and place in a salad bowl. Chop onion very finely, toss with lemon juice, and let sit for 10 minutes (Lemon juice mellows the bite of the onion.) Add the cucumbers to the onion. In a separate bowl mix sour cream with white pepper and dill weed, and let sit for 10 minutes. Taste to see if a dash of lemon juice is needed. Add to onions and cucumbers, and gently toss together.

Distribute on 4 salad plates, garnish each plate with one sprig or blossom of dill, and sprinkle with a little paprika to give it a touch of color.

Dessert: Peach Mousse

Ingredients (serves 4):
2 lbs peaches fresh or canned
1 Tbsp lemon juice
½ tsp almond extract
1 cup heavy whipping cream
2 egg whites
⅔ cup + 1 Tbsp (100g) sugar
1 pinch salt

4 fresh mint leaves

Preparation:

Drain canned peaches, or, if fresh peaches, peel, set 1 peach aside, and cut the rest into pieces. Puree peaches in a blender, adding lemon juice, 2/3 cup sugar, and almond extract. Refrigerate for 10 minutes.

In the meantime, whip cream, adding 1 Tbsp sugar, until firm. Set 4 Tbsp whipped cream aside for garnish. Beat egg whites, adding a pinch of salt until peaks are firm. Carefully fold egg whites and rest of whipped cream into peaches, until completely blended.

Spoon into 4 dessert cups. Refrigerate for at least 1 hour. Top with whipped cream and garnish each with a mint leaf and a peach slice.

Note: The easiest way to peel peaches: In a large saucepan, bring water to a boil. Slide peaches into boiling water, one at a time. After about one minute, the skin will start to fold. Remove the peaches with a slotted spoon, and hold briefly under cold water to cool. Now the skin can be peeled off easily.

Special dish of the month: Mini meatloaves in mushroom sauce

Meat loaves were very popular in postwar Germany. Ground meat was cheap and could be transformed into hundreds of delicious dishes — and my mom sure knew how to perform that transformation. My family used to call her "the Leftover Queen" and she was proud of that title, too. So here's one of my favorites that I still do today. I prefer half pork and half beef meat.

Ingredients (serves 4):
1½ lbs ground meat
1½ dinner rolls or 3 slices white bread (one day old)
1 large onion
2 eggs
2 crushed garlic cloves
1 tsp marjoram
Salt, pepper to taste
1 tsp chopped parsley
Breadcrumbs
2 Tbsp clarified butter
or 1 Tbsp peanut oil
and 1 Tbsp butter

For the sauce:
1 cup mushrooms, thinly sliced and tightly packed
1 Tbsp finely chopped onion
2 Tbsp butter
2/3 cup heavy cream
2/3 cup beef broth or 1/3 cup broth and 1/3 cup beer
2/3 cup half & half
1 Tbsp flour
Salt to taste
Freshly ground pepper to taste
4 tsp chopped parsley
dash of lemon juice

Preparation:

To make meat loaves, finely chop the onion, sauté in hot oil and let cool. Soak dinner rolls or white bread in cold water. Using a cheesecloth, squeeze water out thoroughly, then pass through a sieve or grinder, or mash with a fork. Combine ground meat, rolls, eggs, sautéed onion, 1-2 Tbsp breadcrumbs, garlic, marjoram, salt, and pepper, and blend well. Wet hands and form into small loaves. Roll loaves in breadcrumbs to coat all sides. In a frying pan, bring butter or peanut oil to medium heat. Fry meatloaves on all sides until golden brown, and they are done. Set aside and keep warm. Keep drippings in the pan for the sauce.

To make the sauce, add butter to the pan containing the drippings, add a pinch of sugar, and stir until foamy. Lightly sauté the onion, then add the mushrooms, cook briefly and season with salt and pepper. Add heavy cream and beef broth, and bring to a boil. Mix the flour and the half & half, and stir into the sauce. Bring again to a boil, and cook, constantly stirring, until sauce is thick and creamy. Finish with chopped parsley, lemon juice, if needed, and salt and pepper to taste.

Spoon sauce on 4 dinner plates and top with the meat loaves.

Recommended side dish: Our carrot potato dish (see January menu) or pasta and mushrooms.

I prefer a red wine like Cabernet Sauvignon with this dish.

Note: I usually fry these meat loaves in 1 Tbsp clarified butter and 1 Tbsp peanut oil. This way the butter doesn't burn. And if you don't want to use too much heavy cream, you can replace the half & half with 2% milk. I love adding a little amount of beer to the sauce; it gives it a different taste.

My favorite mushrooms are chanterelles (Pfifferlinge) unfortunately not available in the United States, so a picture has to suffice.

September in the Ahr Valley

Ahr Valley seen from the Vineyards

September in the Ahr Valley

I love this valley for its steep hills and beautiful hiking trails through the vineyards. The Ahr river valley is one of the not-so-secret-anymore tourist venues for (red) wine lovers, especially for those who love to hike and bicycle. And in addition to wine and wine festivals, you also find beautiful small towns, cities, churches and houses, with a history going back about 2,000 years.

The city of Remagen on the confluence of Rhine and Ahr, for example, was founded by the Romans around 50 A.D., and they called it Rigomagus. In 1980, the city established the Friedens Museum (Peace Museum) in the towers of the Bridge at Remagen, built in 1916-18. This bridge became famous in World War II as the last remaining bridge over the Rhine that, in 1945, Allied troops were able to cross during their advance on Berlin.

The Ahr Valley is also Germany's most Northern wine growing area. The river has created a beautiful valley in this part of the Eifel area, just southwest of Bonn. People have used the valley's slopes to produce what I think are some of the finest red wines I've ever tasted. Germany is famous for its white wines (some say serve as the country's viticultural ambassadors around the world.) It is lesser-known for its red wines, which I highly recommend trying. And the Ahr River Valley is a red wine lover's paradise.

Also a paradise for hikers, especially in summer and fall, the vineyards are teeming with people walking, bicycling, and enjoying wine and snacks at the wayside rest places. At its peak in fall, when vineyards and forests are showing off their colors, and wine festivals take place every weekend, the area is filled with tourists coming from all over Europe. Signposts showing a cluster of red grapes signal two scenic routes through the region. The "Rotweinstrasse" (red wine trail) for motorists is a beautiful scenic drive, and the "Rotweinwanderweg" (red wine hikers' trail) goes all the way into the Eifel hills.

70 *Pictures from top right clockwise: Remagen bridge, rest area on Red Wine Trail, Ahrweiler houses, typical little chapel along the way, Coffee and Cake sign, winery, on the Red Wine Trail, on the river, typical town scene, area maps*

Cyclists can also discover the region's wines and hospitality by following the "Ahr-Radtour," a well-marked loop trail, beginning at Remagen and circling back to the Rhine. And those who run out of steam can return by train because bicycles "ride" for free. We hiked from Ahrweiler on the slopes of the valley all the way to the end, the source of the river, then took the train back, not for free, though — a wonderful adventure.

The three-day Wine Market in Ahrweiler, a medieval town at the heart of the Ahr Valley, is held every May and offers a good overview of the region's wines. The city's historical market square turns into a bustling, open-air tasting room, where visitors can sample dozens of regional wines served in cute little shot glasses. These tastings are a rare treat since these wines are only produced in very small quantities. Most of them are only available locally, and never make it to the national market. The "Spätburgunder" (German Red Burgundy, the literal translation would be Late Burgundy.)

About the Menu

Onion pie and young wine, called "Federweisser" (which translates to "feather white",) is part of the traditional beginning of the wine harvest season. And hiking the wine country (like the Ahr River Valley, west of Frankfurt,) is a real treat. In the Alsace area of France, a very similar wine "companion" is known as Flammekuche (flaming cake.) Flammekuche recipes have various fillings, but the basic recipe includes sour cream, onion, and bacon.

For the start of the mushroom season, I have a wonderful mushroom soup to whet the appetite. After that, I offer a traditional recipe for partridge (Cornish game hen does as well,) which is a little different from how Minnesotans prepare a partridge. As this dish is sided with sauerkraut, there is no need for a side salad, but I didn't want to miss sharing this recipe with you. To learn more about mushrooms in Europe, see page 108.

Our dessert again is focused on what we can do with our favorite red wines – here red Burgundy, but a red Zinfandel (one of my favorite wines) works wonderfully as well.

I know rabbit is not one of the common meats in our country, but German (and European) cooks just love rabbit dishes. You cook rabbit in white or red wine, depending on where you go. Here is our family version and I promise it's good.

September in the Ahr Valley

Appetizer:
Zwiebelkuchen, Onion pie

Soup:
Mushroom cream soup

Entrée:
Pheasant or Cornish game hen on wine sauerkraut with mashed potatoes

Side salad:
Mixed greens with chives cream

Dessert:
Pears in red Burgundy wine or a chocolate mousse

Beverage:
Red Zinfandel or Shiraz

Special dish of the month:
Rabbit in white wine sauce sided with Karin's potato gratin

And it's plum harvest time,
don't forget to add plums to the Rumtopf

Appetizer: Zwiebelkuchen (onion pie)

Ingredients (serves 4):

For the pie crust:
2/3 cup +1 Tbsp (150 g) Quark or Ricotta
5 Tbsp milk
5 Tbsp vegetable oil
1 1/3 cup (300 g) flour
1 tsp baking powder
1 pinch of salt

For the filling:
2 lbs + 1 cup (1 kg) onions, peeled and thinly sliced
1 cup (100 g) thickly sliced bacon, diced
1 Tbsp vegetable oil
2 cups (1/2 l) sour cream
2 eggs
1 tsp flour
1 tsp salt or to taste
1/2 Tbsp cumin
1 pinch freshly ground black pepper

Preparation:
Blend pie crust ingredients carefully, form ball, place in a bowl, cover with a towel and refrigerate for 30 minutes. Put dough on a greased cookie sheet, and pat down to fit the entire cookie sheet, including a little rim.

Sauté bacon in 1 Tbsp oil until transparent. Drain but reserve drippings. Mix 2 Tbsp drippings with sour cream and eggs, stir in 1 tsp flour and blend well. Evenly distribute onion slices on dough, sprinkle with bacon pieces, cumin, salt and pepper. Pour sour cream mixture on top.

Place cookie sheet in the cold oven, set heat to 400°F (200°C) and bake for about 30–40 minutes. The pie is done when the top is nicely browned, and a wooden toothpick comes out clean.

Note: This recipe is calculated for a pizza cookie sheet but could be downsized to a 9" pie pan. However, if using a 9" pan, cut ingredients in half. And if you don't have time to make the pie crust from scratch, use a frozen pie crust. It's not as good as this one, but it works well, too.

Soup: Mushroom cream soup

Ingredients (serves 4):
1 lb mushrooms, (baby portobellos, criminis, or any other kind)
2 Tbsp butter
1 Tbsp sifted flour
Salt and freshly ground black pepper
Pinch nutmeg
1/2 tsp dried marjoram
3 1/2 cups chicken broth
1/2 cup sour cream
1 Tbsp fresh chives, cut into thin rolls
1 Tbsp chopped fresh parsley

Preparation:
Brush mushrooms clean with dry paper towels, or wash quickly, and pat dry. Cut off stems, and cut into thin strips. In a big saucepan, melt butter, season with salt and pepper, and sauté mushrooms, stirring, until all liquid has evaporated. Dust with 1 Tbsp flour, and add cold chicken broth. Bring to a boil, stirring frequently. Add sour cream, marjoram, nutmeg, and salt and pepper to taste. Simmer for another 5 minutes. Serve sprinkled with chives and parsley, along with French bread.

Note: If you like this soup a little thicker and creamier, mix 1 tsp cornstarch with 1 Tbsp milk, and slowly add to simmering soup, stirring constantly. And you can use more flour in the first place if you want to.

I like to sauté a finely sliced onion and a mashed garlic clove with the mushrooms as a variation of this recipe.

Entrée: Pheasant or Cornish game hen with wine sauerkraut and Portobello mashed potatoes

Ingredients (serves 4):
2 young pheasants or Cornish game hens (about 2 lbs)
2 Tbsp brandy
Salt and freshly ground black pepper
8 juniper berries
4 slices bacon
2 Tbsp sunflower oil
2/3 cup sour cream
1 cup white wine
2 carrots
1 medium onion
1 rib celery

Preparation:
Preheat oven to 425°F (225°C.) Pour 2 Tbsp sunflower oil into a casserole and place in oven. Wash pheasants or Cornish game hen thoroughly, pat dry, and rinse inside with brandy. Rub with salt and pepper inside and outside. Crush juniper berries and rub on the outside of the birds. Cover breast parts with bacon slices, tying cooking twine around to secure them, and bind together legs and wings. Brown pheasant in casserole pan.

Meanwhile, peel and dice carrots, onions and celery, and add to casserole. After about 30 minutes, add white wine. Roast for about 50 minutes, basting birds frequently with pan sauce.

When birds are done, remove from oven. Pour sauce through a sieve, covered with cheesecloth, into a saucepan. Bring to a boil, and add sour cream, and salt and pepper to taste. Remove twine from birds and cut into serving pieces.

Side dish: Portobello mashed potatoes

Ingredients (serves 4):
2 lbs potatoes
2 Tbsp butter
1 cup milk
Pinch of nutmeg
Salt and white pepper
½ cup dried portobello mushrooms, soaked in boiling water for 30 minutes

Preparation:
Peel and quarter potatoes. In a saucepan, bring enough water to a boil to cover potatoes. Add 1 tsp salt, and boil potatoes until tender. Remove from pan and let dry.

Meanwhile, in a separate saucepan, bring milk, butter and nutmeg to a boil. Drain soaked mushrooms, but reserve soaking liquid.

Puree mushrooms in a blender. Add pureed mushrooms to milk, add potatoes, and mash well. To achieve a smooth consistency (to your taste and liking,) you can add small portions of the mushrooms' soaking liquid, and whisk potatoes until fluffy. Add salt and white pepper, to taste, before serving.

Side dish: Wine sauerkraut with grapes

Ingredients (serves 4):
1 onion
1 Tbsp sunflower oil
2 cans (8 ounces each) drained sauerkraut
1 cup seedless green grapes quartered
1 cup champagne or fizzy wine (Riesling works as well)
2 cloves
1 bay leaf
Salt and white pepper to taste

Preparation
Peel and finely chop onion. In a saucepan, heat oil to medium heat and sauté onion until transparent. Loosen the sauerkraut, with a fork, and then add it to the onion. Stir in wine, cloves and bay leaf. Cover, reduce heat, and simmer for about 15 – 20 minutes or until sauerkraut is tender. About a minute before the sauerkraut is done, stir in grapes, and let sit to warm them. Add salt and pepper to taste, before serving.

Note: If the sauerkraut is too salty or sour, drain the liquid first, then let the sauerkraut sit in cold water for 2 hours, and drain again, before using.

Beverage: Red Zinfandel or Shiraz

Side salad: Mixed greens with cream of chives

Ingredients (serves 4):
4 cups fresh mixed salad greens
2 pieces white toast without crust, 1 day old, diced
1 cup milk
2 hard-boiled eggs, finely chopped
½ cup hot water
¾ cup vegetable oil
1 tsp mustard
1 lemon zest
1 Tbsp lemon juice
¼ tsp sugar
Pepper and salt to taste
2 cups fresh chives, thinly sliced
4 tsp chives, thinly sliced

Preparation:
Soak bread in milk for 30 minutes. Add eggs and puree in food processor. Add rest of ingredients, except chives and slowly puree. Pour mixture into a bowl, add 2 cups of sliced chives, and mix well.

Place mixed greens on 4 salad plates, top with chives cream, garnish 1 tsp sliced chives.

Note: This is an excellent salad dressing, but it is also a good accompaniment for cooked meat, and can serve as a great dip for vegetables.

Dessert: Pears sautéed in red Burgundy wine

Ingredients (serves 4):
4 pears
2 cups red Burgundy wine
½ cup brown sugar
½ cup water
½ stick cinnamon or ½ tsp ground cinnamon
1 grated zest of lemon
4 mint sprigs for garnish

Preparation:
Peel pears, core, and cut into halves. In a saucepan, bring red wine and other ingredients to a boil. Immediately reduce heat to a simmer. Add pears, and simmer about 12 minutes, until pears are tender, but not mushy. Remove saucepan from heat. When cool, remove pears from saucepan and place on separate glass dessert plates. Bring wine sauce to a boil again, reduce heat, and reduce the sauce to half the quantity. Remove cinnamon stick and pour sauce through a sieve that has been covered with cheesecloth. Let cool, and serve pears topped with sauce and a little sprig of mint as a garnish.

Note: If you need to save time or want more liquid sauce, don't simmer the sauce. Instead, stir in ½ Tbsp cornstarch diluted in 1 Tbsp cold water and bring to a boil.

I have tried other red wines like Pinot Noir and Merlot, but I prefer a softer wine, like Burgundy or red Zinfandel.

Alternative dessert: Chocolate mousse

Do you feel more like having a nice, sweet chocolate mousse or cream for dessert? Here is one of my favorite chocolate recipes that I'd like to share with you. My friend Brigitte from France gave it to me. While raising three children, she always knew how to bring something yummy to the table that didn't take a lot of effort, but still made her family happy.

And you can find lots of different recipes for chocolate mousse, some of them adding 4 ounces of butter to the chocolate melt, or ground black pepper, cinnamon, strong espresso, vanilla or more sugar, or all of the above together. I prefer this one, though, because it is light, and I can eat it without feeling guilty. Enjoy…

Ingredients (serves 4):
1 bar (4 ounces) of dark baking chocolate
4 eggs, separated
⅔ cup + 1 Tbsp powdered sugar

Preparation:
Beat egg whites with powdered sugar until peaks are very stiff. Bring a saucepan of water to a boil, place another pan inside, and melt chocolate in this pan, stirring frequently. Remove pan with chocolate from heat, cool for 2 minutes, then fold in egg yolks slowly and carefully. Then fold in the egg whites with a spoon, until all is blended well. Refrigerate overnight. The mousse will have a firm consistency the next day.

Note: An alternative to the double boiler procedure would be to use microwavable chocolate fudge. Use according to instructions, and proceed with recipe as described above. However, I prefer the taste of this dark chocolate. I achieve my best results using Ghirardelli 70% baking chocolate.

Special dish of the month: Rabbit in white wine sauce, paired with Karin's potato gratin

Yes, I have noticed that many people in the United States don't consider rabbits food. Europeans, on the other side, have developed a culture of cooking them in a variety of ways. They

cook them in white or red wine, sweet and sour, hearty, creamy, ragout style (Minnesota hot-dish,) in pieces with vegetables, or serve the whole little beast. You name it — the recipe is out there.

In Germany and France, you'd find another member of the rabbit family, the hare (Hase.) I have seen there is a black hare in California, called a Jackrabbit. However, I have yet to find this meat for sale in our local stores. In Europe, the hare has a specific hunting season and is considered "game," like pheasant, boar and deer. It is prepared like deer and boar, with a dark sauce or as a sweet and sour dish called "Hasenpfeffer" (see recipe in the December menu.) I grew up with "Hasenpfeffer" (translated hare pepper) as a special dish for a winter holiday.

The rabbit is the domesticated variety of the hare family and kept not only for its nutritional value. Much as in our country it is a pet, a "bunny," cute and fluffy. Follow my advice: if you decide to prepare this dish, don't tell your children that it's a bunny rabbit.

A little story on the side: during WWII, when there was not enough food available, people would eat cats, and call them "Dachhasen," (translated "roof hares") — no kidding.

I like this rabbit recipe because it's easily made and delicious.

The white wine in this recipe can be replaced with red wine, like Pinot Noir, but then you'd have to replace the white wine vinegar with red balsamic vinegar.

Ingredients (serves 4):
1 rabbit or 3 lbs rabbit cut into 4 pieces, washed and dried

For the marinade:
1 cup (1 Glas) dry white wine, like Pinot Grigio
1 Tbsp white wine vinegar
3 Tbsp grapeseed or olive oil
1 medium onion, coarsely chopped
1 tsp dried thyme
1 bay leaf
2 tsp chopped parsley
1 tsp salt
1 tsp black peppercorns

For the roast:
½ cup (125g) lean bacon slices, diced
2 cups water
1 Tbsp butter
1½ cup (200g) finely sliced onions
1/3 cup (75g) finely chopped shallots
1 clove finely chopped garlic
2 Tbsp flour
1 cup (1 Glas) dry white wine, like Pinot Grigio
1 cup (1 Tasse) beef broth
1 bouquet garni of 1 sprig parsley, 1 bay leaf, and 1 sprig thyme

Note: In Germany, "bouquet garni" is the name for a bunch of herbs, usually thyme, parsley, and bay leaf, tied together, and used to cook the meat, then removed after cooking.

Preparation:
Preheat oven to 355°F (180°C)

In a large saucepan, mix marinade ingredients and add rabbit pieces. Cover and refrigerate overnight or for at least 12 hours, turning rabbit pieces several times. The next day, cook diced bacon in boiling water for 5 minutes. Remove from heat and drain.

In a saucepan, melt butter over medium heat, and cook bacon pieces until golden brown. Remove bacon and cook onion slices in drippings until golden brown. Set aside for later use.

Remove rabbit pieces from marinade and pat dry, reserving marinade for later use. Brown rabbit pieces in drippings with onion slices, remove and place in an oven-proof baking dish.

In a separate saucepan, roast shallots and garlic, dust with flour, and add wine and broth. Stir constantly, cooking until the sauce is thick. Pour sauce over the rabbit pieces, add bouquet garni and bacon pieces, pour in the marinade, and bake in preheated oven for 50–60 minutes.

After the first 30 minutes, add the onion slices. When ready to serve, remove bouquet garni, and add pepper and salt, as well as vinegar, to taste. Serve with noodles or potatoes, and a side of mixed greens.

Note: This dish is best served with the same wine variety you have used to prepare it.

Side dish: Karin's potato gratin

Ingredients (serves 4):
1 lb (450g) yellow potatoes
2 cups bacon or cooked ham finely diced
1 cup heavy whipping cream
1 cup sour cream
1 cup milk
Salt and white pepper, to taste

Preparation:
Peel potatoes and slice very thin, almost like shaving. Cook bacon in a saucepan. Drain drippings into a container and set aside. Using a paper towel, rub the bottom of an oven-proof 9" baking dish with bacon drippings.

Place 1/3 of the potato slices in the baking dish, in an overlapping pattern. Mix the whipping cream, sour cream, milk, pepper, and salt. Pour 1/3 of the cream mixture over the potatoes. Repeat layers twice more.

Place baking dish in the cold oven, set to 350°F (175°C,) and bake until the top of the potatoes is golden brown, the potatoes are tender, and the cream is very thick.

Did You Know? Potatoes ...

Potatoes had been popular in Europe since 1536 when Spanish conquistadores brought them back from their conquest of South America. Incas and other South American peoples had cultivated the "papa" from 8,000 to 5,000 B.C. Within a few decades, potatoes spread throughout Europe and became a staple for the rich and the poor.

King Frederik II, the Great, was known to literally beat his subjects into accepting the potatoes as nutrition. Until this time, people did not accept potatoes as something they could eat. Legend has it that he had his soldiers guard a potato field to make his farmers believe the incredible value of these plants.

In Switzerland, potato plants were first cultivated for the beauty of their blossoms, only later for their nutritional value. In Ireland, potatoes were highly regarded, as they took little effort to grow, harvest and cook. Thrown into the peat fires around the houses, they quickly made a healthy meal.

In the 1840s, a plant disease, the potato blight, wiped out the crops in Ireland and Northern Europe, leading to the "Potato Famine" and, consequently many families emigrated from their homes and came to North America.

Potatoes arrived in the North American colonies in 1621 when the governor of Bermuda sent two large cedar chests with potatoes and other vegetables to the governor of Virginia. The first permanent potato fields, however, were established in New Hampshire by Irish immigrants, and from there spread all over the country.

A few fun facts:

During the Alaskan Klondike gold rush, potatoes were practically worth their weight in gold, for their nutritional value, and gold was more plentiful than nutritious foods.

In 1995, the potato was the first vegetable grown in space. NASA and the University of Wisconsin created the technology to be able to feed astronauts on long space travels.

The Incas placed raw slices of potatoes on broken bones to promote healing; measured time by correlating units of time to how long it took for potatoes to cook; treated facial blemishes by washing their faces with cool potato juice; treated frostbite or sunburn by applying raw grated potatoes to the affected areas, or eased a sore throat by putting a slice of baked potato in a stocking, which they tied around the neck.

French agronomist and pharmacist Parmentier helped King Louis XIV popularize the potato in France in the 18th century. Parmentier created a feast with only potato dishes, a concept he realized was possible when he was imprisoned in Germany and fed only potatoes. Benjamin Franklin, when he was the ambassador to France, was in attendance of Parmentier's feast in 1767. Colleague Thomas Jefferson introduced deep-fried potatoes as French Fries during his presidency at the White House.

In 1853, railroad magnate Commodore Cornelius Vanderbilt complained that his potatoes were cut too thick and sent them back to the kitchen at a fashionable resort in Saratoga Springs, NY. To spite his haughty guest, Chef George Crum sliced some potatoes paper thin, fried them in hot oil, salted and served them. To everyone's surprise, Vanderbilt loved his "Saratoga Crunch Chips," and potato chips have been popular ever since.

And yes, there is a Potato Museum in Blackfoot/ Idaho.

October in the Eifel Mountains

Bad Münstereifel, a typical Eifel Town

October in the Eifel Mountains

The Eifel is the region between the Mosel River in the South and the Rhine river in the East, formed by volcanoes long ago. Its mountainous part around Daun and Manderscheid, which is called the "Vulkaneifel" (the volcanic Eifel,) is now a National Park. Eifel's main industry is tourism: people come to see the beauty of its hills, valleys, and its famous "Maare." These almost perfectly round lakes, deep, dark and cold developed over the millennia, as the volcanic hills flattened by erosion, the craters sank, and ground water filled them. The water of the Eifel, another important part of the region's industry, are famous. The mineral water of Gerolstein is a major article of global export. People from all over come to visit the spa cities of Bad Münstereifel, Daun, Manderscheid and others. They hope to cure their illnesses with the help of the region's water and its excellent air.

The Eifel region has been important since Roman times because of its central location between the waterways of four rivers. The Lords of the area of Saar-Mosel-Ruwer, and the Rhine were able to control much of the trade routes along these rivers. And when the Roman population left 400 years later, they left behind a culture of wine growing, churches, monasteries, and cities throughout the region, some of them still standing. The monastery of Maria Laach is not only an important station on the Camino de Santiago (St. James pilgrimage way,) but also famous for its Gregorian chant music performances. The shell of St. James is the marker for this pilgrimage way. This way is still very active. You find the shell on houses and churches in cities all over Europe to the Spanish city of Santiago de Compostela (and it looks very much like the Shell company's shell.)

Most Formula 1 car racing fans probably know the racing track "Nürburging," close to the town of Adenau. Notorious for its dangerous North loop, this race track was made safer a few years ago.

Pictures from top right clockwise: Manderscheid Castle, Bad Münstereifel, Daun, Cloister Maria Laach, St. James Pilgrimage Way sign, mushroom heaven, Nürburgring Formula 1 race track, Totenmaar, Rurtalsperre Recreational area, area maps

I have fond memories of the Nürburgring events: we used to set up tent villages for our traditional May 1st pilgrimage to the hilltop. We would stay overnight in the cold, build huge bonfires to keep us warm (and sometimes catch "the" cold of the year,) and then cheer for our champions the next day. There was not much to see when they roared by — but it was a great adventure.

With its abundance of water, the Eifel area offers yet another industry for the good of its people. The Nazi regime built the area's first dams, creating a huge industry of energy production. However, despite these dams, the lakes allow the tourist industry to flourish with boating, swimming, and surfing, as well as hiking and biking. And when you drive into the small villages and towns in the Eifel, you see many signs of "Zimmer Frei" (Bed & Breakfast,) to attract visitors.

Fall is my favorite season in the Eifel. I used to make a yearly trip to the quaint city of Monschau, with its surrounding majestic beech forests ablaze with fall colors.

About the Menu

Mushrooms are a delicacy in Germany, and fall is the best season to gather them. When I grew up, my family used to vacation in the Eifel area. The owner of "our" little hotel would invite us children to go with her "into the mushrooms" (early in the morning at 5 a.m.) She would teach us to distinguish between boletes, criminis and chanterelles, and also their poisonous relatives.

Going "into the mushrooms" on the European continent was, and still is, a sport, like going hunting and fishing in Minnesota. Pharmacies have pictures in their outside windows. They also have mushroom experts inside who can assist amateur mushroom hunters to define the value of their "prey," thus guaranteeing the safety of their lives (also see page 108.) And during Fall you see the "hunters" with their baskets going into the woods of Germany, France, Belgium, Italy and Spain to find their prized trophy mushrooms.

Of course, the safe way is to buy them at the markets. Come October, the markets are overflowing with boletes, chanterelles, morels and other kinds found in the woods. The cute little fellow on the right is a fly agaric mushroom (Fliegenpilz,) easily identified by its red cap and white spots. This one is just bad for your well-being, but other kinds like the "Knollenblätterpilz" (it resembles a chanterelle and cannot be found in the U.S.) are deadly!

October in the Eifel Mountains

Appetizer:
Pasta salad with white crab meat

Soup:
Pumpkin soup with julienne of leek and carrot

Entrée:
Mushroom ragout in Pfannekuchen
(German pancakes)

Side salad:
Spinach salad or romaine lettuce with
lemon and tarragon dressing

Dessert:
Zwetschgenkuchen (Plumcake)

Beverage:
Merlot or Pilsner beer

Special dish of the month:
Pork fillet in beer sauce with
apples and cranberries or a
ide dish of spicy stewed dried fruit compote

Rumtopf reminder: Add pears to your delight

Appetizer: Pasta salad with white crab meat

No family party went without Mom's famous pasta salad, and this is an adaptation of it. Instead of diced wieners I use crab meat and replace the onions with the same amount of celery. I think Mom would love this variation, too. And I love her variation, but have not found the "right" Wieners yet.

Ingredients (serves 4):
2 cans of white crab meat drained and flaked with a fork
1 rib celery finely diced
1 medium tomato, seeded, and finely diced
2 cups of cooked small bow-tie or elbow pasta
2 Tbsp sour cream
Salt and white pepper, to taste
1-2 Tbsp Tarragon vinegar
Paprika powder for garnish
4 leaves of curly endive for garnish
4 sprigs of parsley for garnish

Preparation:
Mix crab meat, celery, tomato and cooked pasta in a bowl. Mix the dressing ingredients in the salad bowl, adding enough vinegar to give it a tangy touch. Fold pasta mixture into the dressing and add salt and pepper to taste. You can also spice it up with a little touch of curry if you like that.

Place 1 leaf of lettuce on each of 4 salad plates, and spoon a portion of salad onto each leaf. Dust each salad with a pinch of paprika (for a touch of color,) garnish with sprigs of parsley, and keep refrigerated until ready to serve.

Note: White crab meat is available in most grocery stores. If you can't find it, however, 2 cups of finely chopped cooked shrimp will not taste as well, but will be adequate. And if you can't find tarragon vinegar, use white wine vinegar and add ½ tsp dried tarragon leaves.

Soup: Pumpkin soup with julienne of leek and carrot

Ingredients (serves 4):
1 pumpkin (about 2½ lbs, or 1 kg)
2 cups vegetable or chicken broth
2 cloves of garlic
1 small onion
4 Tbsp butter
1 cup (1/4 l) dry white wine, like Pinot Grigio
2 Tbsp sour cream or heavy cream
Salt and freshly ground black pepper
1 pinch of cayenne pepper
½ tsp dried or freshly chopped ginger
2 carrots
1 stalk of leek
2 Tbsp butter

Preparation:
Peel pumpkin, remove seeds, and cut pumpkin into 1" pieces. Peel and finely chop onion and garlic. In a large saucepan, melt butter, and sauté onion and garlic until transparent. Add pumpkin pieces, stir to coat, and sauté for about 5-10 minutes, until tender.

Add broth and simmer for 15 minutes. Stir in white wine, and bring to a boil. Remove from heat and blend in a blender, until creamy. Pour back into the saucepan, add cream (sour, or sweet, as you like it,) add spices to your taste, and bring to a simmer. While the soup is simmering, clean and julienne carrot and leek into thin strips. Sauté in melted butter until they have browned just a little bit but are still al dente.

Ladle soup into 4 soup cups (as an appetizer) or bowls (as entrée,) and sprinkle with the julienned vegetable. For additional garnish, you could sprinkle ½ tsp very finely chopped parsley around the edges of the soup bowl. Serve with crisp French bread.

Entrée: Mushroom ragout with Pfannekuchen (German pancakes)

In vegetarian circles, mushrooms are acclaimed as the "meat of the vegetarian," especially the boletes (the porcini mush¬rooms.)

I have grilled boletes in butter in a pan over medium heat, first dipping them in beaten egg, then coating them with a mixture of breadcrumbs and grated Parmesan cheese. I fried them until they turned golden brown. Served with a tomato sauce and red wine they are just delicious. That would be Italian style, seen in the area of Lake Garda. This recipe, however, is my grandmother's version and my favorite.

Ingredients (serves 4):
2 lbs (1 Kg) mushrooms like boletes, chanterelles, criminis or portobello mushrooms
4 Tbsp butter
3 medium sized yellow onions, finely chopped
1 finely diced carrot
1 finely diced rib celery
1 finely chopped clove garlic
4 dried morels
1 cup red wine
1 cup beef bouillon

1 tsp salt
pinch freshly ground black pepper
½ tsp dried thyme
1 pinch sugar
1 Tbsp tomato paste

Preparation:
Soak dried morels in 1 cup boiling water for about 30 minutes. Clean fresh mushrooms with a paper towel (Don't wash them under running water.) Trim stems, or, if necessary, remove stems. Cut mushrooms into 1" size pieces.

In a saucepan, melt 3 Tbsp butter over medium heat. Add onion, carrot, celery and garlic, and cook until onion is transparent. Do not brown. Stir in mushrooms, reduce heat, and simmer, occasionally stirring, until mushrooms are tender. Set aside.

In a separate large saucepan, melt 1 Tbsp butter. Add sugar and stir until sugar caramelizes, add red wine and stir until well blended. Stir in mushroom mixture, and add tomato paste, stirring until blended. Pour morel broth through a sieve into the saucepan, always stirring, and add beef bouillon, pepper, salt, and thyme. Simmer about 15 minutes, until sauce has thickened.

Make 4 pancakes according to recipe on next page. Place a pancake on each dinner plate. Spoon mushroom ragout onto half of the pancake, and fold over the other half. Garnish with a sprig if thyme, or parsley.

Note: You could replace boletes with Portobello mushrooms. They are not as tasty, but it'll be alright.

Pfannekuchen (German pancakes)

This dish goes well with a spinach salad. However, here I'd like to give another option, a simple green lettuce salad with lemon dressing. Pfanne¬kuchen is often served as a full entrée in traditional restaurants. A good "Speckpfannekuchen" (bacon pancake) or "Apfelpfannekuchen" (apple pancake) is the pride of the chef, and that restaurant can easily become a popular venue.

Ingredients (serves 4):
1 cup of flour
2 cups of 2% milk (or 1 cup each skim milk and half & half)
2 eggs
pinch of salt
white pepper to taste
pinch of sugar
8 Tbsp butter (1 stick)

Preparation:
Mix ingredients in a blender. Follow the above order, because otherwise you'll get clumps. Let sit for about 30 minutes. In a 9" frying pan, melt 2 Tbsp butter for each pancake. Set heat to medium heat, pour ¼ of the batter into the pan, and cook until the bottom of the pancake is golden brown, probably with darker spots. You should be able to lift the pancake with a spatula. When ready, flip the pancake over and cook until the bottom is also nicely golden brown. Usually, little bubbles will appear, and I leave them. Some people prick them open with a fork or the tip of a knife. Set pancake in a warm oven, and repeat procedure with the other three pancakes.

Note: Some chefs replace the milk with beer, which gives the pancakes a hearty taste. French crepes are made that way, too.

Side salad: Romaine lettuce with lemon tarragon dressing

Ingredients (serves 4):
1 garlic clove peeled and cut in half
4 cups romaine lettuce
3 Tbsp sunflower oil
3 Tbsp lemon juice + 1 Tbsp cold water
½ tsp salt or more, depending on the acidity of the lemon juice
1 pinch white pepper
1 Tbsp dried chervil or tarragon

Preparation
Rub inside of large salad bowl with the inside of garlic cloves. Mix lemon dressing ingredients in the bowl, add romaine lettuce and toss carefully until all is coated.

Beverage: Red wine like Merlot or Pilsner beer

Dessert: Dorothea's Pflaumenkuchen (Plumcake)

There are several recipes for Germany's traditional and famous plum cake. This one, Dorothea's recipe, is the most common yeast dough plum cake. "Pflaumen" (plums) are also called Zwetschgen.

Ingredients (serves 4):
1 package of yeast dough, ready made
2 lbs plums, pitted, and cut almost in halves, but with the halves still connected on one side
1 cup granulated sugar
1 cup powdered sugar
1 cup heavy cream
1 Tbsp sugar, or enough to sweeten it to your taste

Preparation:
Preheat oven to 425°F (220°C) On a cookie sheet, roll out dough. Place plums on top, with the connected side down. Sprinkle with granulated sugar. Bake for about 30 minutes. Cool and then sprinkle with powdered sugar. Beat heavy cream until stiff. Place pieces of cake on dessert plates, and top with whipped cream.

Special dish of the month: Pork tenderloin in beer sauce with apples and cranberries, dried fruit compote or creamed savoy cabbage

Ingredients (serves 4):
2 medium sized tart apples, washed, cored and cut in half
4 Tbsp cooked cranberries
2 peeled and thinly sliced onions
4 pork fillets (about 6 ounces each and about 1" thick)
pinch salt
pinch freshly ground black pepper
2 Tbsp flour divided
1 Tbsp butter
1¼ cups amber beer
1¼ cups sour cream

Preparation:
Preheat oven to 450°F (230°C)

Place apple halves in an ovenproof dish. Bake for 5 minutes in preheated oven. Remove from oven, and fill with cranberries. Salt and pepper pork fillets and dust with 1 Tbsp flour. Heat butter in a skillet to medium heat and brown pork fillets for about 5 minutes on each side. Add onion rings and sauté pork fillets and onion rings together until pork is almost done. Remove from pan and keep warm. Set pan on heat again, add the beer and bring to a boil. Mix 1 Tbsp flour with sour cream, and add to the beer. Reduce heat, and simmer for about 1 minute or until sauce thickens, stirring constantly.

Spoon 2 Tbsp sauce on 4 dinner plates, place pork chops on top, set a filled apple next to pork chop. Serve the hot sauce in a separate bowl.

Serve with baked or steamed potatoes or creamed savoy cabbage and a Pilsner or the same amber beer you used for the sauce.

Alternative side dishes

Side dish: Dried fruit compote
Another delicacy I remember in my parents' home was a side dish of dried apricots, apples, and prunes.

(Serves 4)

Cook 4 cups of dried fruit (your choice.) in 6 cups of water. Add sugar, salt and pepper to taste, and maybe a chopped onion and 1 Tbsp white vinegar, if you like. Cook until fruit has regained all its juices and is almost like a hot chutney, but not as spicy.

Goes well with the pork tenderloin (or any pork dish) instead of the apples, but is also delicious just served with noodles.

Side dish: Creamed Savoy cabbage
This more "normal" side dish goes very well with the pork fillets and the beer sauce, just in case you don't like the fruity approach.

Ingredients (serves 4):
1 savoy cabbage, deveined, and chopped into bite-size pieces
1 cup sour cream
½ Tbsp salt
1 pinch white pepper or to taste
1 pinch sugar
½ tsp cumin
1 Tbsp butter

Preparation
Melt butter in a saucepan over medium heat. Add sugar, and stir to caramelize. Stir in chopped cabbage, pepper, salt, and cumin, and sauté until cabbage is tender. Add sour cream, and, if necessary, add a little more, so cabbage has a creamy consistency. Add more salt and pepper to taste, if needed.

Serve with pork fillets, instead of apples or compote.

November on the Baltic Sea

Fish Trawler in Warnemünde Old Harbor

November on the Baltic Sea

This part of Germany was not accessible until 1989, when "The Wall" and the "Iron Curtain" came down.

Since then it became one of my favorite places to visit. Mecklenburg–Vorpommern and the Baltic Sea are beautiful, with steep bluffs and chalk cliffs, the contrast of dark pine trees against white beaches showing off their fine sand dunes. Swimming on these beaches is safe at almost any time, as the Baltic Sea has no tides. The mainland, the Lake District around the capital city of Schwerin, has flat woodland, hills up to 540 feet, and the beauty of about 2,000 lakes. The Elbe and Warnow rivers serve as waterways for commercial shipping and recreational boating, and the state is full of National and State parks, forests and lakes, a paradise for city dwellers and nature seekers.

The history of this area goes back about 10,000 years. Archeologists excavated communities and settlements dating back as far as 1800 B.C. Later on, Vikings and Slavs built settlements, fortresses and trade centers. The Slavs moved on when German immigrants came from the West in the 13th century. In the 14th century, the Dukes of Mecklenburg reigned, but after the religious wars in the 17th century the country was handed over to the Swedish crown. In the Middle Ages, the cities of the Hanse, the Hanseatic League, were very influential and made this area a center of trade and economical and political power. After WWII, it became part of the USSR's German Democratic Republic, and since The Wall came down in 1989, the region has slowly been recovering from the devastation of its Communist regime.

Nautical-based industries — ship building and fishing — have always been the major source of income in this region, and since the times of the Hanse, it has been a center for nautical trade and fish exports. Today, however, about 1/3 of the state's area is used for agriculture. Tourism has been here since the 19th century, with famous spa towns like Heiligendamm. This town is well-known as the "white" resort town, which, in its heyday, hosted royalty and celebrities from all over Europe.

Pictures from top right clockwise: Warnemünde lighthouse, Daarst old house, Warnemünde Captains' houses, Rostock Hanse architecture, Rostock University, sunset on the Baltic Sea, Heiligendamm beach scene, Bad Doberan train "Molli," Heiligendamm Spa "White City," area maps

Today, it is being rebuilt to its old splendor with hotels, spas, and beaches surrounded by its lovely cliffs.

The harbor city of Warnemuende, where the Warnow river flows into the Baltic Sea, is one of the most beautiful old German resorts on the Baltic coast. It is famous for its fine beaches, old captains' houses and quaint restaurants. It is also famous as one of the best regatta areas in Europe. We fell in love with the idyllic "Old River" with its sailing boats, pleasure ships and fishermen selling the catch of the day, and loved the charming small boutiques and fishermen's pubs and the promenade along the Baltic shoreline. From there we could watch, directly from the pier, big luxury cruise ships, sailing vessels, ferry boats, and freighters entering and leaving the harbor.

Another not-to-miss trip is to Bad Doberan, where a narrow-gauge railway, lovingly called the "Molli," is still in use. Molli goes through the middle of town and is the normal means of public transportation to the spa resort of Kühlungsborn. Love it.

A source from the 16th century describes the people living in this area as "a people careful in one's speech, who hates lies and flattery, but loves to have guests and be a guest" and we found this to be true. An area to revisit.

About the Menu

This beet and orange appetizer is one of my husband's favorites. It combines all the flavors — sweet, tart and spicy — and is always a hit at a dinner party.

Fish and a green salad with lemon dressing, or a cucumber salad with dill dressing, are wonderful companions. However, as this area of Germany is famous for its potatoes, my salad this month is a potato salad, which could be used as an appetizer as well.

The fish ragout contains potatoes, but sometimes I just leave them out and have potato salad on the side. Or I just skip any salad and have French bread on the side.

My grandma used to make bread pudding from leftover stale bread. A few days ago, I sampled a bread pudding dessert in a restaurant in Minnesota, and it reminded me of my grandma's dessert. After some searching through her old recipe book, I found this recipe, which is different from the traditional way of cooking a pudding. I have made it with and without apples, and it is great both ways.

Beef loin with fruit like plums and apples is a traditional dish in Mecklenburg. Rumor has it that Germany's Chancellor, Angela Merkel (from this area) has a particular liking for this specialty.

November on the Baltic Sea

Appetizer:
Beets and Oranges with an orange and horseradish cream dressing

Soup:
Herbed soup

Entrée:
Mecklenburg fish ragout

Side salad:
Biedermeier potato salad

Dessert:
Bread pudding or wine cream

Beverage:
Gewürztraminer or Sauvignon Blanc

Special dish of the month:
Gundula's beef loin with apples, plums and potatoes

Last but not least — Apples for the Rumtopf, the last fruit to join the crowd.

Appetizer: Beets and Oranges with an orange and horseradish cream dressing

Ingredients (serves 4):
8 small beetroots, unpeeled
4 oranges
4 sprigs of parsley

For the dressing:
Grated zest of 1 orange or 1 tsp dried orange zest
1 cup of frozen orange juice
1 Tbsp orange liqueur (Cointreau or Triple Sec)
dash Angostura bitter
Salt and white pepper to taste
7 Tbsp Mayonaise
1 tsp horseradish or to taste

Preparation:
Cook beets in water until tender. (Use a spoon and press down to test.) Drain, rinse under cold water, and let cool for about 5 minutes. Rub peel off, using a paper towel, and slice each into 3 slices. Cut each orange into 3 slices crosswise, and cut off the peel. Blend all ingredients for the dressing in a separate bowl.

Ladle 3 Tbsp of dressing on each of 4 salad plates. Place the slices of orange in a circle on each plate, and then arrange beet slices on top. You should have 3 oranges slices and 6 beet slices for each portion. Garnish with a sprig of parsley or the top of a green onion, sliced lengthwise.

Note: Although I am reluctant to name a brand in this book, my choice of bitter for this dressing would be Angostura bitter. And you can, of course, use canned beets, but it's not the same delicate taste.

Soup: Herbed soup

Ingredients (serves 4):
4 cups of mixed fresh herbs like dill, celery leaves, leek, parsley, chives, and sorrel or arugula
2 Tbsp butter
1 Tbsp flour
4 cups chicken broth or beef broth
Pepper, salt
Nutmeg
2 Tbsp sour cream
4 sprigs of parsley

Preparation:
Wash and dry herbs, then chop finely. In a saucepan, melt butter over medium heat. Add flour and, combine with butter until creamy, frequently stirring. Add ¼ of the chopped herbs. Add broth, constantly stirring, and bring to a boil. Reduce heat and simmer for about 5 minutes. Add pepper, salt and nutmeg to taste.

Just before serving, stir in the remaining ¾ of the herbs, and the sour cream.

Ladle into 4 soup cups, and top each one with 1 sprig of parsley.

Note: I have tried this soup with arugula only, and it is delicious, too.

Entrée: Mecklenburg fish ragout

Ingredients (serves 4):
5 onions
1 cucumber
8 Tbsp butter or, preferably, drippings
1 clove garlic
4 medium sized potatoes
1½ lbs white fish fillet of your choice
1 pint of hot chicken or beef broth
1 Tbsp medium hot mustard
1 bunch dill, fresh and chopped, or ½ cup dried dill
2 Tbsp tarragon, chopped, or 1 Tbsp dried tarragon
1 cup half & half
1 tsp lemon juice
1 Tbsp white wine
Salt and pepper

Preparation:
Peel onions, cucumber and potatoes, and cut into ¼ inch pieces. Crush garlic. Cut fish fillets into 1-inch pieces, and lightly salt pieces. Steam potatoes until almost done. In a large saucepan, over medium heat, melt butter, and add garlic, onions, and cucumbers. Sauté quickly. Add potatoes, fish pieces, and add hot broth, reduce heat and simmer for about 15 minutes. Just before serving, add mustard, dill, and tarragon. Remove saucepan from heat, stir in half & half and, as the finishing touch, add lemon juice and/or white wine to taste.

Note: This normally would be paired with a salad of fresh greens like the one on page 83 and a beer. I prefer the white wine I use for the ragout.

Beverage: Gewürztraminer or Sauvignon Blanc

Side salad: Biedermeier potato salad

Ingredients (serves 4):
1 lb potatoes, steamed and cut into ½" cubes
1 cup sweet pea pods
½ English cucumber seeded and cut into ½" cubes
1 cup fresh green asparagus tips, steamed but not mushy
2 tomatoes, seeded and cut into ½" pieces
For the dressing:
1 small onion, thinly sliced or chopped
4 Tbsp vinegar, preferably white wine vinegar
1 cup vegetable oil (I love this salad made with grape seed oil)
Salt and pepper to taste
pinch of sugar
1 Tbsp finely chopped parsley
1 Tbsp finely chopped lovage
1 Tbsp finely chopped tarragon
Some parsley sprigs for garnish

Preparation:
Combine potatoes, pea pods, cucumber, asparagus, tomatoes and onion in a large bowl. In a separate bowl, mix dressing ingredients together. Add to salad and toss gently to coat. Let sit for 1 hour outside of refrigerator before serving. Garnish with parsley.

Note: If you want to replace the fresh tomatoes with diced canned tomatoes, that's alright. Just make sure they are thoroughly drained. My favorite adaptation of grandma's recipe is this: I use canned vegetables like sweet corn and peas, replace the cucumber with pickles, and the tomatoes with red bell peppers or carrots, all finely diced. (I use whatever is in my fridge.)

Dessert: Bread pudding or wine cream

Ingredients (serves 4):
1½ cups (300 g) whole grain bread crumbs
1 cup white wine or milk
1 cup water
½ cup (120 g) raisins
2 Tbsp sugar
Cinnamon sugar (1 Tbsp sugar + ½ tsp ground cinnamon, mixed)
2 Tbsp frozen butter
4 tart apples peeled and cored, cut into thin slices
1 Tbsp breadcrumbs

Preparation:
Preheat oven to 400°F (220°C)

If you don't have breadcrumbs already, grate 2-day-old bread and, in a shallow plate, drizzle with water and wine or milk. Soak raisins in hot water for about 30 minutes. Butter a shallow, oven-proof baking dish.

Put in a layer of breadcrumbs, top with apples, sprinkle with raisins, and cinnamon sugar to taste, and finish with another layer of breadcrumbs. Shave frozen butter flakes on top, and sprinkle again with 1 Tbsp of breadcrumbs. Bake in preheated oven for about 60 minutes. Remove from oven and keep warm until served. Serve with vanilla sauce.

Note: My family made this kind of bread pudding with Schwarzbrot. And they didn't add apples, but apples give this recipe a wonderful taste, especially when served with vanilla sauce. You can also serve any ready-made vanilla sauce or vanilla yogurt with this dessert.

Alternative Dessert: Wine Cream

Ingredients (serves 4):
3 envelopes gelatin (Knox seems to be the only brand available)
½ cup orange juice (1 medium sized orange)
4 egg yolks
1 lemon zest
¾ cup (200g) sugar
⅓ cup lemon juice (1 medium sized lemon)
1 cup plus 1 Tbsp (250 ml) strong white wine, like Chardonnay
1 cup + 1 Tbsp (250 ml) heavy whipping cream
8 seedless grapes, halved
4 sprigs of fresh mint

Preparation:
Whip cream until peaks are stiff. Set aside 4 Tbsp whipped cream for garnish. Mix egg yolks with sugar, lemon zest, lemon juice and wine, and beat or whisk until well blended. In a double boiler bring water to a boil. Place bowl with egg mixture into boiling water. Heat mixture until it rises, beating or whisking mixture constantly, remove the bowl from the water and set aside. In a large bowl, sprinkle gelatin over the cold orange juice, and let sit for 1 minute. Slowly add hot egg mixture, and whisk until gelatin is completely dissolved, which may take up to 5 minutes. Let cool, stirring frequently. When it starts to thicken, carefully fold in whipped cream.

Rinse 4 dessert bowls or champagne glasses with cold water and sprinkle with sugar. Pour in dessert and refrigerate until it is firm. Garnish each bowl with 1 Tbsp whipped cream, 4 grape halves, and a sprig of mint.

Note: Gelatin (see also chapter Ingredients) is a commonly used ingredient in German cooking. It is used for desserts and appetizers like Beef Aspic. It can be found in almost all supermarkets and grocery stores. Make sure you get the original, unflavored product.

Special dish of the month: Gundula's beef loin with apples, plums, and potatoes

A very traditional dish, in Mecklenburg, is my girlfriend Gundula's family recipe: beef loin with prunes. I remember my mom making something like this, although not with beef, but with pork. That was wonderful as well. In Mecklenburg, this dish would be paired with boiled potatoes. I have tried this with noodles and liked it very much.

The Northern part of Germany on the Baltic as well as the North Sea also has some very interesting (and sometimes very different) dishes that combine fish, meat, fruit, and vegetables. One of them is the Labskaus, famous in the Hamburg area. I like this one because the prunes and apples are a wonderful addition to the beef flavor.

And my favorite beverage with this would be a Merlot, although, according to Gundula, the traditional beverage would have been a light beer.

You will need to start preparing this dish the day before the dinner

Ingredients (serves 4):
12 ounce (about 350 g) prunes, soaked a day ahead of time
5 ounce (150 g) tart apples
2½ lbs beef loin
1 cup (200 g) soup vegetables (celeriac, leek, carrot,) diced
6 black peppercorns
½ tsp salt
2 bay leaves
1 onion, diced
For the sauce:
4 Tbsp butter
2 finely chopped onions
2 Tbsp flour
1 pint of beef broth, using the cooking broth from the beef loin
Salt and pepper to taste
1 cup chopped parsley

Preparation:
The day before the dinner, soak prunes in 1 quart of water. The next day, bring 2 quarts water, the beef loin, spices, and vegetables in a large pot to a boil. Remove foam, reduce heat, and simmer, covered, for about 70 minutes. Remove vegetables. Peel and cut apples into pieces. Add apples and prunes, including soaking water, bring to a boil again, reduce heat, and simmer uncovered for another 20 minutes.

To make the sauce, melt butter in a saucepan, over medium heat. Add onions and cook until transparent. Add flour and stir until the mixture is golden colored. Carefully add hot beef broth, one spoon at a time, constantly stirring. Bring to a boil, simmer for about 20 minutes. Add pepper and salt to taste, and sprinkle with chopped parsley.

Remove beef from broth, and cut into slices about 1" thick. Place on individual dinner plates or a big serving plate. Ladle sauce on top and place prunes around it.

Serve with potatoes, peeled and steamed, or in boiled in salt water.

December at the Christmas Markets

Traditional Christmas Market in Dresden

December at the Christmas Markets

Oh yes, December in Germany is a good time! We like these Christmas markets with their huts, gifts, Christmas ornaments, Glühwein, Bratwurst, and Reibekuchen. Children play Christmas music in house entrances, and choirs sing from the balconies of administration buildings (yes, all outside)! Too bad there is not as much snow in Germany as there used to be; that would improve the ambiance even more. The good news is it is seldom really cold.

Most people who have been to Germany know the Nürnberg Christkind'l Market, one of the first of its kind. Today, you can find Christmas markets in almost every city. A sort of "Christmas Market tourism tradition" has developed with tours to the better-known markets of Berlin, Munich, Cologne, Frankfurt, Nürnberg, Dresden, and Düsseldorf. Düsseldorf, where the market extends throughout the inner city and Old Town is quite an experience. Personally, I prefer the smaller markets of towns like Kleve or Idstein because of their quaint surroundings. I have found that markets in these small, old towns attract more artists and are not yet as commercial as are many of the bigger cities' markets.

An Advent wreath is a very German tradition: on the first Sunday of Advent, four Sundays before Christmas Eve, the first candle of the Advent wreath is lit. The next Sunday we light another candle and the next, and on the fourth Sunday all candles are lit.

Germany has a counterpart of America's Santa Claus, St. Nikolaus. In the Roman Empire, around 300 A.D., a bishop named Nikolaus was famous for generously giving gifts. For us children, one of the highlights of Advent was Nikolaustag (St. Nicholaus' Day) on the 6th of December. In the old days, on Nikolausabend, (Nikolaus Eve, the 5th of December,) children left hay and straw for St. Nicholaus' horses. We, as city children, simply sat a shoe or boot outside of our bedroom door for the Holy Man to fill.

I remember the visits of St. Nikolaus, when I was a child. My dad, disguised as the Holy Man, would come

Pictures from top right clockwise: children playing carols, Idstein, Düsseldorf Christmas Carnival, Cologne, Advent wreath, Dresden Meissen, Düsseldorf, St. Nikolaus on Neuss Christmas market

in with a big "Ho-ho," we sat on his lap and had to tell him about our sins during the past year. His companion was "Knecht Ruprecht," his ugly and nasty servant, who used to threaten to beat us children with his bundle of twigs if we hadn't been good. But that never happened. We had all been angels all year long, of course.

Traditionally, Germans celebrate their Christmas, called "Heiligabend" (Holy Night,) on Christmas Eve. The Christmas tree will have been cut down or purchased and decorated just a few days earlier, and the lights are lit for the first time this evening. As children, we had to recite or play the Christmas story and sing Christmas carols while my mom in the adjacent room, behind closed doors, lit candles on tables piled high with our presents. When we heard a faint ding-a-ling of bells ringing, we knew the Christkind (Christ child) had made his visit. Then the door opened, and there were the gifts we couldn't wait to open. Everybody, even the parents, had a Christmas basket with oranges, nuts, apples and candy, and we would munch on them over the next few days. Yes, in the 1950s, that was still something very special in Germany. Fond memories.

About the Menu

December at the Christmas Markets

"Reibekuchen" (potato pancakes) are an indispensable ingredient of any good German Christmas market. Usually, it is the famous "Glühwein," the German spiced wine that goes with it.

In fine German cooking, sherry wine has an important role. It is used for sauces, soups and salad dressings to give them the final, "fine" touch. Here we add sherry to our appetizer and soup.

Winter in Germany is not what it used to be. Very seldom do temperatures go below freezing, and it can be pretty rainy and drizzly in the north, especially in the Rhineland area.

Christmas time also is hunting time and the time to buy fresh game items in the markets. Traditionally, my family had this entrée as our Christmas Day special dinner, and we sided it with an apple sauce and cranberries that accompany the "Sauerbraten." My mother didn't side venison with "Semmelknödel" (bread dumplings); she preferred boiled potatoes. I got this dumpling recipe from friends in the Nuremberg area, where this is the preferred side dish.

The baked apples are a dessert that I loved to make in the evening, sometimes even as a full meal, for myself. Just having the house filled with the aroma and perfume of apples, cinnamon and vanilla gives one the feeling of Christmas.

December at the Christmas Markets

Appetizer:
Bean salad with shrimp in a vinaigrette

Soup:
Creamed Tomato soup with sherry

Entrée:
Loin of venison with Brussels sprouts and Semmelknödel" (bread dumplings)

Side salad:
Arugula salad with vinaigrette, cranberries and walnuts

Dessert:
Baked apples in vanilla sauce
Christmas treat: Spekulatius

Beverage:
Pinot Noir or a red Burgundy (if you can find it, try a German Spätburgunder)

Special dish:
Reibekuchen (Potato pancakes) with Glühwein (spiced red wine)

Hasenpfeffer, another traditional family Christmas recipe

Time to enjoy your Rumtopf—with a scoop of vanilla ice cream or vanilla pudding

Appetizer: Bean salad and shrimp with a lime vinaigrette

Ingredients (serves 4):

2/3 cup (150 g) small cooked shrimp, fresh or frozen and thawed
7 ounce (200 g) fine green beans (haricots)
4 sprigs of parsley
For the vinaigrette:
2 limes, cut into thin slices
2 finely chopped shallots
½ bunch finely chopped parsley
3 mint leaves
3 basil leaves
3 Tbsp white balsamic vinegar
4 Tbsp extra virgin olive oil
½ tsp salt
2 Tbsp sherry
pinch cayenne pepper

Preparation:
In a bowl, mix ingredients for the dressing. Let sit covered for 60 minutes before serving. Steam beans until tender, but still al dente. Decorate 4 salad plates with slices of limes. Place beans on top, then top with shrimp. Drizzle with dressing and garnish with parsley.

Note: You can mix the beans and shrimp, and top them with limes, too, instead of layering them. That is just a matter of presentation, and your personal preference.

Soup: Creamed Tomato soup with sherry wine

Ingredients (serves 4):

¼ cup (250 ml) diced bacon
1 small onion, chopped
1 Tbsp vegetable oil (sunflower, canola, etc.)
1 16 ounces can (500 ml) pureed tomato sauce
1 cup (250 ml) beef broth
½ tsp sugar
3 Tbsp sherry wine or 2 tsp red balsamic vinegar
Freshly ground black pepper and salt to taste
4 Tbsp heavy whipping cream, lightly beaten
4 leaves chopped parsley or basil cut into strips

Preparation:
In a saucepan, heat oil to high heat. Sauté bacon in oil until cooked, but not crisp. Reduce heat to medium, add onions, and sauté until transparent. Add tomato sauce and broth. Cook for about 5 minutes. Add salt, pepper and sugar to taste. Remove from heat, and add sherry or vinegar. (Add vinegar just one tsp at a time, until you like the taste.)

Ladle soup into 4 soup dishes (or cups or bowls.) Beat heavy cream until it is semi-firm. Place one Tbsp whipped cream on each soup dish, and lightly swirl around the surface. Place one teaspoon of chopped parsley or a few strips of basil leaves in the middle of each soup serving. Serve with toasted French bread.

Note: If you like croutons, you could place croutons in the middle of the soup's surface, instead of parsley.

Entrée: Loin of deer/venison with Brussels sprouts and Semmelknödel (bread dumplings)

Ingredients (serves 4):

2½ lbs deer/venison loin, without bones
2 Tbsp vegetable oil (peanut oil or sunflower oil)
2 Tbsp butter
Salt and pepper
1 peeled and diced onion
1 peeled and diced carrot
1 leek, cleaned and diced
¼ peeled and diced celery root (celeriac)
2 cups (500 ml) red wine
1 cup (250 ml) beef broth
3 Tbsp butter
2 Tbsp flour
2 Tbsp cranberry jelly or cranberries

Preparation:
Set oven to lowest temperature

In a large roaster, bring vegetable oil to medium-high heat, then add the butter. Add vegetables and cook until onion is transparent.

Place deer loin in a roaster and brown on all sides.

Reduce heat, add wine and broth, and cook, covered, for about 90 minutes. Test with a wooden pick to see if the meat is done. Remove from heat, and place loin, covered with a tent of aluminum foil, in the oven to keep warm. Don't wrap completely: it should not cook anymore.

Pour the contents of the roaster through a sieve into another saucepan, reserving the liquid, but discard vegetables. Bring liquid to a boil again and continue to simmer.

In a separate saucepan, melt butter over medium heat. Add flour and constantly stir until it has a creamy, dark brown consistency. Add ½ tsp sugar, stir, and slowly add the liquid from the roaster.

Bring to a boil, then reduce heat and simmer, uncovered, for about 20 minutes. Add a little salt and pepper, to taste, and add sour cream and cranberry jelly, or cranberries. If the sauce seems too thick, add tablespoons of broth as needed until sauce has a smooth consistency.

Serve with dumplings and steamed Brussels sprouts.

Note: If you don't want to use red wine, replace it with 2 more cups of beef broth and 1 tsp balsamic vinegar

Side dish: Brussels sprouts

Ingredients (serves 4)
1 lb Brussels sprouts
2 Tbsp butter
1 pinch salt

Preparation:
Clean Brussels sprouts. Bring salted water to a boil, and stir in butter. Add Brussels sprouts and cook until done but still al dente.

Note: I like to add butter or peanut oil because it brings out the flavor of almost any vegetable in a very delicate way.

Side dish: Semmelknödel (bread dumplings)

Ingredients (serves 4):
3 stale breakfast rolls or slices of toast
2 Tbsp flour
Salt
2 Tbsp bread crumbs
3 Tbsp butter
3 eggs

Preparation:
Soak rolls or bread in water, press water out and pass through a sieve or a blender.

Mix flour, salt, and bread crumbs. In a saucepan, melt butter over medium heat and add bread mixture. Constantly stir mixture until it forms a ball. Remove from heat and immediately stir in one egg. Set aside to cool. After about 10 minutes, add 2 additional eggs, and let sit for about 10 minutes to let the dough rise.

In a large saucepan, bring 2 quarts of water to a boil. Reduce heat to a simmer.

Dip 2 spoons in the hot water and form little dumplings. Drop dumplings into boiling water and simmer for 10 – 15 minutes. Using a slotted spoon, remove dumplings and serve with deer loin. Bread dumplings go well with other meat dishes or a mushroom sauce, too.

Side salad: Arugula salad with vinaigrette, cranberries and walnuts

Ingredients (serves 4):
4 cups of arugula (stems trimmed)
4 Tbsp chopped walnuts
1 cup dried cranberries, soaked for 30 minutes, drained
For the dressing:
4 Tbsp walnut oil
2 Tbsp white wine vinegar
1 – 2 Tbsp lemon juice
1 pinch each of ground red pepper, paprika, nutmeg & coriander
Pepper and salt to taste (use a little more salt to counter¬act the acidity of the lemon.) I like to add a little chili pepper.

Preparation:
In a large bowl, mix dressing ingredients. Wash and dry arugula and add to vinaigrette. Toss gently to coat all. Divide among 4 salad plates and sprinkle with walnuts and cranberries.

Note: Although here the preparation is a salad, arugula is also worth trying as a vegetable or in soup.

Beverage: Pinot Noir or a Red Burgundy
(If you can find it try a German Spätburgunder.)

Dessert: Baked apples in vanilla sauce

Ingredients (serves 4):
4 large, tart apples, washed and cored
For the filling:
4 Tbsp sugar
2 Tbsp raisins, soaked in water for about 30 minutes
1 tsp cinnamon
1 Tbsp melted butter
2 Tbsp sliced almonds

4 small pieces of cold butter

Preparation:
Preheat oven to 350°F (220°C)

When coring the apple, don't cut all the way through, so that there's a little bottom left. Drain raisins and discard water.

Mix all ingredients for the filling. Place the apples upright in a large, buttered baking dish. Carefully spoon the filling into the cores of the apples. Top each apple filling with a little slice of cold butter. In preheated oven, bake 25-45 minutes, depending on the size of the apples. Apples should be tender when tested with a toothpick. Serve with vanilla sauce.

Note: I recommend buying a vanilla sauce instead of making it from scratch, but I'll include the recipe below.

Vanilla sauce from scratch

Although I loved the taste and the result, I hated to make this sauce. Why? I was the one who had to whisk the liquid, and make sure that the milk would not boil over and burn. So today you'd have to pay me to make this wonderful sauce from scratch, although nothing can beat this great taste!

Ingredients (serves 4):
3 cups milk or half & half
1 Tbsp vanilla extract or, preferably, 1 vanilla bean
¼ cup sugar
1 egg
2 egg yolks
1 Tbsp corn starch

Preparation:
Set aside 2 Tbsp milk. Slice vanilla bean and scratch out the seeds. Pour the rest of the milk into a saucepan, and add vanilla seeds and the empty vanilla bean. Or if you use vanilla extract, just add that to the milk. Bring to a boil, let rise once, remove saucepan from heat and set aside. Remove vanilla bean, if you used one.

Beat sugar with egg and egg yolks until foamy. Blend 2 Tbsp milk (the ones you had set aside) with corn starch. Constantly stirring add the sugar-egg and cornstarch mixtures to the milk in the saucepan, and bring to a boil again. (Don't stop stirring.) Remove from heat and let cool. While sauce is cooling down, keep stirring now and then.

Note: I like ground vanilla extract that I have recently found in co-op markets in the U.S. The difference between the real vanilla, and the artificial flavor is remarkable!

A little Christmas treat: Spekulatius cookies

Spekulatius cookies are as inseparable from German Christmas as the turkey is from our Thanksgiving. So here's the finest version, the Mandelspekulatius (Almond Spekulatius cookies.) Spekulatius is baked using special cookie forms called "Model." You probably won't find these special forms in the U.S., so you can cut the cookies into forms to your liking, but pat them very flat. By the way, I found this wooden model on EBay, but it's only on the German website and only for delivery in Germany.

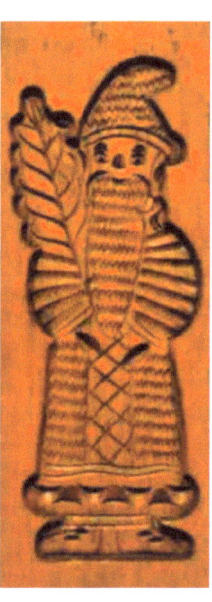

Ingredients (makes about 70):
1 lb flour
8 ounces butter
2/3 cup sugar
½ cup ground almonds
2 eggs
1 package vanilla sugar (see Note)
1 pinch cinnamon
1 pinch salt
1 pinch powdered cloves
1 cup or more sliced almonds

Preparation:
Preheat oven to 400°F (200°C)

In a large bowl, mix all ingredients thoroughly. Refrigerate for 60 minutes. On a cookie board, roll dough out very thinly (about 1/4" (2 mm) thick,) then cut into forms, using a cookie cutter.

Place cookies on a lightly buttered cookie sheet, and sprinkle with almond slices. In preheated oven, bake for 10-15 minutes, until golden brown on top.

Note: In some supermarkets, you can buy Dr. Oetker vanilla sugar, a mix of ground vanilla and sugar. You can make your own by mixing 1 tsp sugar and ½ tsp vanilla extract.

Special dish: Reibekuchen (potato pancakes) and Glühwein

A German Christmas market without Reibekuchen and Glühwein is unthinkable. And in the Rhineland area, Reibekuchen are served either topped with sugar or with a side of apple sauce. As you have seen, apple sauce is an important ingredient in Rhineland cuisine. Particularly important in the Rhineland version of Reibekuchen is the fact that no flour is used. Consequently, you use fewer eggs, which makes them more crisp and, I think, tastier. The potatoes used to be grated by hand, and in my memory I still see my dad slaving over that chore.

Reibekuchen

Ingredients (serves 4):
1 lb white (Russet) potatoes
1 medium sized onion, finely chopped
1 egg
Bacon drippings or vegetable oil

Preparation:
Grate potatoes into a bowl of cold water. Press grated potatoes through a sieve, making sure they are as dry as possible. Mix potatoes with egg and finely chopped onion.

In a deep pan, bring oil or drippings to medium-high heat. One spoonful at a time, bake Reibekuchen on both sides until they are crisp and golden brown.

Serve sprinkled with sugar (Yes!) and/or sided with apple sauce.

Note: I prefer bacon drippings to vegetable oil for this recipe because it gives the Reibekuchen a more hearty flavor.

Glühwein (German spiced or mulled red wine)

My dad used to say, "Only the best ingredients can provide the best tasting food. You may have the best recipe and skills as a chef, but if you save on the ingredients, you'll be disappointed with the results." I religiously follow his advice, so for this spiced wine, I prefer a good Merlot or Pinot Noir. I have found many recipes for this treat all over Europe and the U.S., but this is how I learned to make it at my parents' home.

Ingredients (serves 4):
1 bottle of good red wine, like Merlot, Pinot Noir or Shiraz
1 cup water
8 cloves
1 cinnamon stick
2 Tbsp sugar, or to taste
1 tsp lemon zest and/or orange zest

Preparation:
In a saucepan, combine water, spices, sugar, and lemon and, if you like it, orange zest, bring to a boil, reduce heat, and simmer for about 15 minutes. Turn off heat, and let sit for about 30 minutes.

Add red wine and carefully reheat on very low heat until almost boiling. Be careful not to let it boil, because the wine would lose its taste. Remove from heat. Let sit for about 2 minutes. Serve in tea glasses, and add sugar to taste, but don't make it too sweet.

Note: If you'd like to make this for your children, use the same proportions, but instead of wine, use apple juice or cider. And since these are sweet already, you don't need to add much sugar.

I love this kind of mulled apple juice in the winter; it warms the bones.

Another Special: Hasenpfeffer (sweet and sour hare,) my family's Christmas dinner

Every year before Christmas, my dad used to go to the farmers' market and buy a hare for our Christmas dinner. It was sold in pieces, ready to use. "Hasenpfeffer" is a traditional dish coming from the Westphalia area, the provenance of his side of the family. This particular recipe was handed down from his grandma to my grandma to my mother to me. I have never tried to prepare it using rabbit because I don't think the taste would be the same.

So here's my family's Christmas dinner dish.

Ingredients:
3 lbs (1½ kg) hare, cut into pieces
½ cup finely chopped onions or shallots
1 cup (250 ml) dry red wine, like Merlot
1 cup (250 ml) chicken bouillon, or better broth
2 Tbsp brandy
10 black peppercorns, crushed
3 Tbsp flour
½ tsp salt
1⅔ cups (400 g) diced bacon
1 tsp red currant jelly
1 small bay leaf

For the sauce:
thyme to taste
2 tsp lemon juice
1 Tbsp flour

Preparation:
Place the hare pieces on a cutting board, sprinkle with salt and pepper, and coat with flour. In a large pan, fry bacon over medium heat until crisp. Remove bacon from pan, leaving drippings in the pan, and place bacon on paper towels to drain. Brown meat pieces in hot bacon drippings, remove from pan, and put on paper towels with the bacon. Pour bacon drippings into a container, keeping 3 Tbsp in the pan. Cook chopped onions in drippings until transparent. Add red wine, chicken broth, brandy, currant jelly, peppercorns and bay leaf, bring to a boil, and reduce heat to simmer. Add bacon and pieces of hare and simmer for about 60 to 90 minutes, until the meat is very tender.

Meanwhile, in a separate saucepan, heat 3 Tbsp drippings, and add flour, constantly stirring. Then stir in 2 cups of cooking broth and salt, thyme, and lemon juice, to taste. Bring to a boil, and remove from heat. Just before the meat pieces are done, pour sauce into the pan with Hasenpfeffer, and mix well.

Serve with red cabbage and potato dumplings or steamed or boiled potatoes.

Note: My grandmother's traditional recipe from her Westphalian home area calls for some blood of the hare to be used for thickening the sauce. And no flour or thyme was used. This dish was also served on Sundays during hare hunting season.

I have never tried it, but I could imagine that this would be a perfect crock-pot recipe. I'd probably cook the stew on low setting for about 10-12 hours or on high for about 8-9 hours.

A Guide to German Food and Beverages

Basic ingredients in German cooking

Soups and sauces

All German soups are prepared with some basic ingredients.

The basic broth or bouillon MUST contain "Suppengrün," a combination of a big carrot, a stalk of leek, a quarter of celery root (celeriac,) and 2 or 3 sprigs of parsley. All vegetables are peeled and cut into large pieces. The parsley only needs to be washed and drained. For chicken broth, you would add a large chicken. Beef broth is normally made by adding a marrow bone to your veggies as well as an appropriate amount of meat.

Vegetables and their Seasons

I grew up in post-WWII Germany, where we didn't have the luxury of everything being available at all times, so the local, seasonal vegetables dictated our diet. In my mind, this is much healthier, too.

I have tried to keep the recipes close to the actual seasons, but rather than being a purist, I have tried to compose menus that worked nicely together.

Celeriac (or celery root or celery knob)

Celeriac is a wonderful vegetable. It is now becoming more popular in the U.S. It doesn't look inviting, but once you have peeled off the dirty, rough exterior, you find an interior that gives soups a wonderful flavor. You can also fry or bake it, use it in salads, or cook it as a side dish in a creamy sauce.

Leek

Leek has a sweet and onion taste at the same time. It is used in soups and as a vegetable, or in pies. Leek is sandy, so the stalks need to be washed with care because they can contain dirt on the inside of their layers. Cut the leek lengthwise to the middle, and open the layers to remove the dirt.

Potatoes

In German cooking, potatoes traditionally are peeled before cooking.. Some families, however, cook the potatoes with peels on, and then remove the peels before serving. Germans call them "Pellkartoffeln," and sometimes serve them with chives cream or butter.

Quark

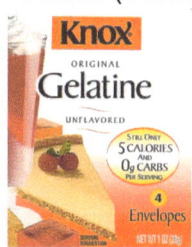

Quark is an important part of German eating. A byproduct of milk (it's like the first step of making cheese,) it's a creamy, smooth white mass, often used in dips, sauces, cakes, desserts, and bread spreads. This versatile, fresh cheese resembles soft cream cheese, Ricotta, or the Mexican soft white cheese. Germans (who call this Quark) and Austrians (who call it Topfen) use it to make everything from cheesecake to gravy. It was hard to find in America; one source was the "Deutsche Haus," and the other was a website in California. Other German ethnic stores might also carry it.

Gelatin (German: Gelantine)

Gelatin is a commonly used ingredient in German cooking for desserts, and appetizers (example Beef Aspic.) Most supermarkets and grocery stores carry them today. You should make sure you get the original, unflavored product.

About American versus German ingredients

I found it out the hard way: flour in America is not the same as in Germany, not to mention the baking powder. Thanks to friends here in the U.S. and back in Germany, I have been able to prepare the German recipes with the ingredients I could find over here. If there had to be a substitute, I mentioned it (like Germany's famous Quark.)

A little guide to commonly used herbs and spices

The German terms are mentioned in parentheses.

Artemisia or mugwort (Beifuss): As this herb helps the body cope with fat meat or fish, it is often used as one of the main ingredients for goose, eel, pork and other fat dishes, but never for vegetables. It has a slightly bitter aftertaste, so you don't want to use a lot.

Arugula (Rukola): Nutty, spicy flavor; add to salads, dips, and stir fry. Try a sauce with arugula pesto to accompany chicken.

Basil (Basilikum): Fresh, sweet, subtle flavor (sometimes a little minty.) Use in tomato and pasta dishes, pesto, and vegetable soups.

Chervil (Kerbel): Add to fish sauces, potato salads, and scrambled eggs. Good for a clear chervil soup.

Chives (Schnittlauch): Mild onion flavor. Use to accent salads, stir fry, omelets and egg dishes. Great for dips as well. Ingredient of sauce for "Tafelspitz."

Cilantro (Koriander): Used for salsa, curry, stir fry, Oriental and Mexican dishes.

Dill (Dill): Light, sweet, dilly flavor. Use in fish sauces, vegetable dips, and serve with fresh potatoes and vegetables.

Garlic (Knoblauch): In traditional German cooking you won't find many recipes using garlic as one of their main ingredients. It has changed over time, though, so today's cooking includes much more Mediterranean flavors than the traditional German recipes.

Garlic Leaf or wild garlic (Baerlauch): Light garlicky taste. Add to sauces and soups, good for dips and sandwiches, great as an addition to sauces for meat.

Lovage, also known as love parsley (Liebstoeckel): Close in taste to tarragon. Also called "Maggikraut" (Maggi herb,) as it's the main ingredient in one of Germany's most famous seasonings, "Maggi."

"Maggi": It's used to spice up soups and sauces. I found it in German ethnic stores and online, too.

Marjoram (Majoran): Add to poultry stuffing, egg dishes, and vegetables.

Mint (Minze): Sweet, fresh spearmint flavor. Use in cool summer drinks, to accentuate new potatoes and salads, and to garnish desserts.

Oregano (Oreganum): Part of the Italian and Greek herb mixture. Used for pasta, spaghetti sauces, pizza, and favorite Italian dishes.

Curly parsley (Krause Petersilie): Good for soups, stews, and for garnish. Especially good after garlic and liquor — chew a few sprigs and your breath is clean again.

Flat parsley (Glatte Petersilie): Also called Italian parsley. It has a more hearty taste than curly parsley. Flavors soups, stews and pasta sauces. Makes great parsley pesto.

Rosemary (Rosmarin): Flavors chicken, marinades, baked meats, and fish. Especially good with lamb. (Try marinated lamb chops on a bed of rosemary, baked in the oven.)

Sage (Salbei): Part of Herbes de Provence. Complements poultry, dressings, sausages, lamb, veal, cheese flavoring, and is great with calf liver.

Sorrel (Sauerampfer): A tart taste to complement cream sauces, fish, salads, and soups.

Tarragon (Estragon): Light anise flavor. Add to vinegar for dressings, chicken ragout (yummy,) and beef stroganoff.

Thyme (Thymian): An ingredient in Italian and French herb mixtures. Necessary for vegetables, soups, and meats.

Watercress (Brunnenkresse): Light, snappy flavor. Accents salads, sandwiches, and clear soups.

About Beers and Wines

The Beers

Beer is still the most popular thirst-quenching alcoholic beverage in Germany, and, like a good wine, you don't want to serve beer too cold; the taste would suffer. Many cities (I only mention well-known ones like Dortmund, Munich, Cologne, Düsseldorf) have their "own" local breweries that have earned a reputation nationwide. Other less-known areas, like the one around Nuremberg in the Franken area, brew wonderful varieties you can only buy locally.

All beers, however, are subject to the "Reinheitsgebot," German purity regulations that date from 1516. They require that German beer can only be produced from 4 ingredients: malt, hops, natural yeast, and water. Let me give you a few examples of well-known beers throughout Germany.

There are two ways of brewing beer: Obergärig (Alt, Kölsch, Berliner Weisse, and Weizenbier) and Untergärig (Lager, Bock, Pilsner.) You cannot tell them apart by color, so here's a listing of German beers by color.

Light-colored beers:

Hefebier: (Paulaner beers from Munich in the U.S. come close)

Helles Bier: Dortmunder Union (U.S. substitute would be a Lager)

Lager beers: Dortmunder Export Bier, a light colored lager

Berliner Weisse: often served with a dash of raspberry or woodruff syrup, fresh and refreshing on hot summer days

Dark-colored beers:

Altbier from the Rhineland area (mostly bitter beers, served in small, straight 8-ounce glasses; I yet have to find it in the U.S.)

Dunkelbier, a dark lager with a more malty taste

Oktoberfest beer, a stronger variation of a dark lager beer

Pilsner: This beer is known in Germany as Pilsener Urquell (originally from the city of Pilsen in today's Czech Republic; more bitter than the same label in the U.S.,) also called Pils.

Here are some facts about German beer from an article written by Robert Easton, "German Beer and the Beer Law," which explains why German beer is different from other beers all over the world. "German beer accounts for about 10% of the worldwide market, and German breweries employ about 65,000 people. There are about 1,200 breweries managing to produce a whopping 5-6,000 varieties. This fact is all the more impressive as the Reinheitsgebot, Germany's Beer Law, restricts brewers to these four basic ingredients. It forbids flavouring beer with any other additives.

The first beer law was laid down in 1487 by Duke Albrecht, who decreed that "a quart of winter beer shall cost one pfennig, a quart of summer beer two pfennigs." He added that brewers "shall take only barley, hops and water for the beer, boil it in a proper fashion, and add nothing else nor permit anyone else to add anything." At that time, they relied entirely on the yeast in the air for fermentation, so brewers did not add the yeast at all. In Bavaria, on the 23rd of April 1516, Duke Wilhelm IV made a similar decree from which the modern law directly descends. Now people mark that day by celebrating German Beer Day on 23rd April every year." And further he writes: "Many Germans believe that the Beer Law makes drinking beer 'purer' and safer because they know exactly what is in their beer." "In fact beer is quite healthy in some respects: one liter of beer contains 45% of the recommended daily allowance of magnesium; 20% of the RDA of potassium, and fewer calories than the same amount of whole milk or grape juice."

And: "Beer, used externally, can also keep your hair healthy, giving it shine and volume. Some researchers found that hops, one of the main ingredients of beer, can help stop the building up of carcinogens in the body."

The Multitude of German Beers

The Wines

Austrian wines don't follow the German wine specifications, so this chapter only refers to German wines. I especially like this website about German wines in the English language. (http://www.e-winegifts.com/german-wine.html)

The Grapes

White wine: Silvaner, Gewürztraminer, Riesling, Weisser Burgunder (White Burgundy, also a Chardonnay grape,) Grauburgunder (Gray Burgundy or Pinot Grigio)

Red wine: Spätburgunder (Red Burgundy)

Rose wine: Spätburgunder Weissherbst (Rose Burgundy)

Red and rose wines come from the Ahr valley and the Pfalz (Palatine) area, white wines traditionally from the Rhine and Mosel–Saar–Ruwer valleys, the Pfalz (Palatine) area in Baden-Wuerttemberg around Landau, the Saxony, Hesse and Thuringia areas.

The following is an excerpt from the German Embassy's website in Washington, D.C. (http://www.germany-info.org):

To learn more about German wines, local vintners open to the public, and wine-related events throughout Germany, the German Wine Institute's website is an excellent place to start. Send for their superb brochures on all wine regions, which include detailed maps and sight-seeing suggestions. For details on visiting the German Wine Roads, including accommodations, restaurants, and noteworthy sights, check out the German National Tourist Board website. For visits to the Rhine wine regions, see this website on the Palatinate region.

Two categories of wine are allowed by the European Union: table wine (Tafelwein, Landwein) and quality wine (Qualitätswein.) The latter category is again subdivided into "b.A." (bestimmte Anbaugebiete, or distinct growing regions.) Light, refreshing, fruity wines meant to be enjoyed young — and "mit Prädikat" — elegant, noble wines well suited to long aging.

"Sekt" is the German equivalent of a Sparkling Wine. However, it is lighter, and fresher than white wine, and has a slightly lower alcohol content.

There are six ascending levels of ripeness and acidity:

Kabinett — elegant wines made from fully ripened grapes; low in alcohol

Spätlese — late harvest wines; balanced, well-rounded, with the intensity of fully ripened grapes

Auslese — noble wines, intense in bouquet and taste, made from very ripe grapes selected in bunches

Beerenauslese (BA) — rare and exquisite wines with the unmistakable honey-like aroma of botrytis ("noble rot",) made from overripe individually selected grapes

Trockenbeerenauslese (TBA) — the crowning achievement of German viticulture; lusciously sweet wine made from individual grapes shriveled almost to raisins

Eiswein — a dessert wine made from grapes of BA quality, harvested and pressed while frozen; remarkable concentration of fruity acidity and sweetness

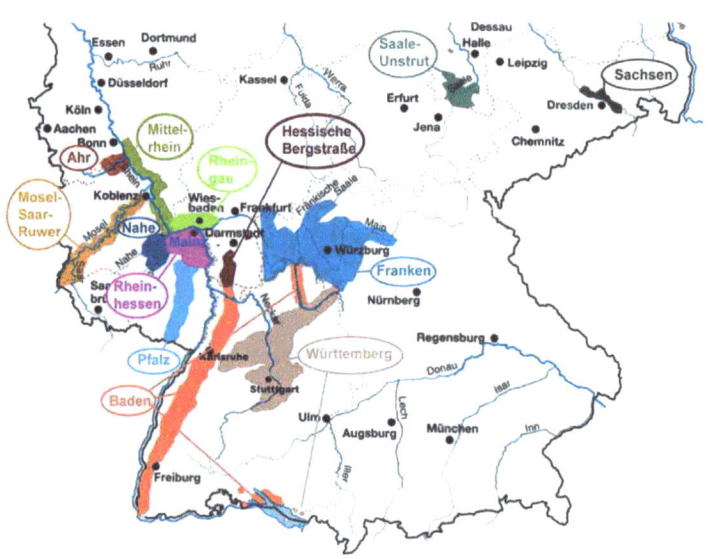

The 13 most important wine-growing areas in Germany

Mushrooms in Europe

As in the U.S., the sort of mushroom used throughout the year would be criminis (Champignons.) However, when the mushroom season starts in September/October, and

the mushroom gatherers go into the woods, the markets are overflowing with boletes, chanterelles, morels and other kinds of these precious little buddies. Going "into the mushrooms" is a sport like going hunting and fishing in Minnesota. Pharmacies have pictures and tables in their outside windows (like the antique poster to the left,) and mushroom experts inside assist amateur mushroom foragers to define the value of their "prey," and guarantee the safety of their lives.

Here is a "short list" of some of the most common mushroom types on German markets.

Criminis are white button mushrooms (Champignons,) generally grown in caves. They are the little button mushroom we can buy in cans.

Chanterelles (Pfifferlinge) are highly favored mushrooms for sauces and ragouts. They make a terrific addition to an egg dish.

Boletos (Steinpilze) are *the* most famous mushrooms (and not easy to find.) They are used dried for sauces, sautéed, grilled like a steak, breaded and baked, in soups and salads. They look like baby Portobellos, but the taste is incomparable.

Morels (Morcheln) are delicious in sauces and ragouts

Portobellos (Wiesenchampignon comes closest) in the "wild" found in meadows, are also grown in caves.

Oyster mushrooms (Austernpilze) are grown in greenhouses and loved in salads and sauces.

And — mushrooms are beautiful.

Dieting?

The sauces making German dishes so delicious are also dangerous for the waistline. Substituting three major ingredients (sugar, wine, and butter) can help.

Substitute sugar and wine: The traditional German way of cooking has been to add a pinch of sugar to most dishes because it brings out the flavor in vegetables and adds color to the sauces. Yummy—but there are people who want it lighter, who need to lose weight. For them, I would recommend replacing sugar and wine in sauces with just a few drops of lemon juice or balsamic vinegar.

Substitute butter: Another part of traditional German cooking is adding butter and cream to the sauces to make them as tasty as possible. The results are, of course, excellent results for the sauce, but not for your cholesterol, or weight. To substitute, use milk or half & half instead of heavy cream, and yogurt or light sour cream instead of Crème Fraiche; each works just fine.

To brown meat without additional fat: If you want to brown meat but don't want to use too much grease or oil, here's the trick. I learned it from my mom after my dad's first heart attack. Brown meat in a non-stick pan over high heat turning it constantly until it has some color. It takes more effort to work this way than browning the meat in butter or oil (and of course, the taste is different,) but it's healthier.

About Lactose and Gluten free sauce:

To achieve a lactose-free sauce: Use 3 Tbsp yogurt mixed with 1 tsp cornstarch to bind it. Add this mixture instead of heavy cream and flour.

Your Notes:

Index

A

Advent wreath   90
Ahrweiler   70
Almond lemon dressing   32
Altbier   99
Angostura bitter   86
Appetizer   9
   Bean salad and shrimp with a lime vinaigrette   92
   Beets and Oranges with an orange and horseradish cream dressing   86
   Belgian endive with mandarin oranges in sour cream dressing   66
   Bell pepper salad   58
   Butter Bean Salad   38
   Celery root (celeriac), fried, in a lemon dressing with walnuts or pumpkin seeds   52
   Cucumber and tomato salad with onions and yogurt dressing   16
   Fennel salad with herbs   30
   Filled Pancake Strips   31
   Leek Quiche   22
   Marinated Salmon à la Ingeborg   44
   Pasta salad with white crab meat   80
   Zwiebelkuchen, Onion pie   72
Apples to the Rumtopf   85
Apricots to the Rumtopf   65
April in the Bergische Land   37
Artemisia   98
Arugula   98
Arugula salad with vinaigrette, cranberries and walnut   93
Asparagus soup   44
Asparagus with melted golden butter, new potatoes, and sliced cooked ham   44
Augusta Treverorum   65
August on the Mosel River   65
Auslese   100
Austernpilze   101

B

Bad Doberan   85
Bad Münstereifel   78
Baerlauch   98
Baked apples in vanilla sauce   93
Baltic Sea   85

Basic ingredients in German cooking   97
   Celeriac (or celery root or celery knob)   97
   Gelatin (German: Gelantine)   97
   Leek   97
   Potatoes   97
   Quark   97
   Soups and sauces   97
   Vegetables and their Seasons   97
Basil   98
Basilikum   98
Bean salad and shrimp with a lime vinaigrette   92
Beef
   Beef loin with apples, plums, and potatoes   88
   Beef loin with horseradish and chives cream   32
   Clear beef bouillon with pancake strips   30
   Meerrettichlende   32
   Tafelspitz   32
Beef loin with apples, plums, and potatoes   88
Beef loin with horseradish and chives cream   32
Beer   67, 98
   Altbier   99
   Berliner Weisse   99
   Bock   99
   Dark colored beers   99
   Dortmunder Export Bier,   99
   Dortmunder Union   99
   Dunkelbier   99
   Hefebier   99
   Kölsch   99
   Kölsch beer   53
   Lager   99
   Lager, substitute for Dortmunder Union beer   99
   Light colored beers   99
   Obergärig   99
   Oktoberfest beer   99
   Pilsner   81, 99
   Reinheitsgebot   99
   Untergärig   99
   Weizenbier   99
Beerenauslese   100
Beets and Oranges with an orange and horseradish cream dressing   86
Beifuss   98
Belgian endive with mandarin oranges in sour cream dressing   66

Bell pepper salad   58
Bergisches Land   36
Berlin   27
Berliner Weisse   99
Beverage
   Beer   17, 67
   Gewürztraminer   87
   Kölsch bee   53
   Merlot   81
   Orvieto   53
   Pilsner   81
   Pilsner or another light beer   15, 17
   Pinot Grigio   53
   Pinot Noir   93
   Red Burgundy   93
   Red Zinfandel   60, 73
   Riesling   67
   Riesling white wine   32
   Sauvignon Blanc   87
   Shiraz   73
   Spätburgunder   93
   White Burgundy   45
   White wine like Chardonnay or Pinot Grigio   39
Biedermeier potato salad   87
Black pudding   54
Bock   99
Boletos   101
Bouillon, chicken   66
Brandenburg Gate, Berlin   27
Bread
   Schwarzbrot (dark whole rye bread)   26
Bread dumplings   92
Bread pudding   87
Brown meat without fat   101
Brunnenkresse   98
Brussels sprouts   92, 93
Burgundy   93
Butter Beans salad   38

C

Cabernet Sauvignon   23
Calf tongue   38
Calf tongue salad with mushrooms   39
Camino de Santiago (St. James pilgrimage way)   78
Carrot and potato dish (Durcheinander)   17
Carrot cream   67

Carrot salad with sweet and sour dressing   45
Cauliflower baked in puff pastry   39
Celeriac (or celery root or celery knob)   97
Celery root (celeriac), fried, in a lemon dressing with walnuts or pumpkin seeds   52
Champignons   101
Chanterelles   101
Chardonnay   39
Charlemagne   42
Cherries to the Rumtopf   51
Cherry Crumble   60
Chervil   98
Chicken bouillon with semolina dumpling   66
Chicken liver   54
Chicken ragout à la Berlin with rice   31
Chives cream   33
Chocolate cake à la Elisabeth   53
Chocolate mousse   74
Christmas cookies: Spekulatius   94
Christmas dinner   96
Christmas markets   90
Christmas treat: Spekulatius cookies   94
Cilantro   98
Cilantro (Koriander)   98
Clear asparagus soup with asparagus pieces   44
Clear beef bouillon with pancake strips   30
Cloister Maria Laach   78
Cochem   65
Cold sweet strawberry soup   39
Cologne   50
Competition between Köln (Cologne) and Düsseldorf   50
Cookies
   Spekulatius   94
Cornish game hen with wine sauerkraut and Portobello mashed potatoes   72
Crab meat   80
Creamed potato soup with leek julienne   38
Creamed Tomato soup with sherry wine   92
Cream of chives   73
Creamy mustard dressing and walnuts   37, 39
Creamy sauce for Matjes   46
Criminis   101

Cucumber and tomato salad with onions and yogurt dressing   16
Cucumber salad in dill dressing   67
Curly parsley   98

D

Dark colored beers   99
    Altbier   99
    Dunkelbier   99
    Oktoberfest bee   99
    Pilsner   99
December at the Christmas Markets   91
Deer, loin   92
Dessert   9
    Baked apples in vanilla sauce   93
    Bread pudding   87
    Cherry Crumble   60
    Chocolate cake à la Elisabeth   53
    Chocolate mousse   74
    Cold sweet strawberry soup   39
    Erdbeerkaltschale   39
    German Cheese Cake with raisins   24
    Kirschmichel (Cherry Crumble)   60
    Mousse of Chocolate   74
    Mousse of peaches   67
    Peach Mousse   67
    Pears sautéed in red Burgundy wine   74
    Pflaumenkuchen (Plumcake)   81
    Reisflammeri   32
    Rhubarb-vanilla cream   45
    Rote Grütze with vanilla ice cream or yogurt cream   17
    Sweet rice in red wine with whipped cream   32
    Vanilla sauce from scratch   94
    Wine Cream   87
    Yogurt Cake   24
    Zwetschgenkuchen   81
"Deutsches Eck" (German Corner) by Koblenz   64
Dieting   101
    Brown meat without fat   101
    Gluten   101
    Lactose   101
    Lactose and Gluten free sauce   101
    Substitute butter   101
    Substitute sugar and wine   101
Dill   98
Dill dressing   67
Dortmunder Export Bier   99
Dortmunder Union   99
Dresden   90
Dressing

Almond lemon dressing   32
Cream of chives   73
Creamy mustard dressing and walnuts   37, 39
Dill dressing   67
Italian dressing   58
Lemon dressing with walnuts or pumpkin seeds   52
Lemon tarragon dressing   81
Lime vinaigrette   92
Mustard dressing   17, 60
Onions and yogurt dressing   16
Orange and horseradish cream dressing   86
Orange-caper dressing   30
Red onion vinaigrette   60
Sour cream dressing   66
Sweet and sour dressing   45
Vinaigrette with cranberries and walnuts   93
Dried fruit compote   82
Dumplings
    Egg Dumplings   58
    Marrow Dumplings   59
    Parsley Dumplings   59
    Semmelknödel (bread dumplings)   93
    Semolina dumplings   66
Dunkelbier   99
Düsseldorf   19, 50
Düsseldorf Christmas Carnival   90

E

Egg Dumplings   58
Eifel region   78
Eiswein   100
Elbe   84
Enjoy your Rumtopf - with a scoop of vanilla ice cream or vanilla puddin   91
Entrée   9, 16
    Chicken ragout à la Berlin with rice   31
    Cornish game hen with wine sauerkraut and Portobello mashed potatoes   72
    Himmel und Erde (Heaven and Earth) with chicken liver or fried black pudding   54
    Kohlrouladen (pigs in a blanket) with potatoes, carrots, and gravy   52
    Loin of deer with Brussels sprouts and Semmelknödel (bread dumplings)   92
    Matjes (young herring fillets) with new potatoes in a creamy sauce   46
    Mecklenburg fish ragout   86
    Mini meatloaves in mushroom sauce   68
    Mushroom ragout with Pfannekuchen (German pancakes)   80
    Mushroom Schnitzel with green beans in creamy mushroom sauce   59

Index

Pheasant or Cornish game hen with wine sauerkraut and Portobello mashed potatoes 72
Ragout from calf tongue with a side dish of cauliflower baked in puff pastry 38
Rouladen (stuffed beef) with a stew of carrots and potatoes "Durcheinander" 16
Sauerbraten with Red Cabbage, Thuringian dumplings and applesauce with cranberries 22
Sole with carrot cream on risotto and kohlrabi 67
White asparagus with melted golden butter, new potatoes, and sliced cooked ham 44

Erbsensuppe (split pea soup) 25
Erdbeerkaltschale 39
Estragon 98
Europe and the European Union 5

F

February in Düsseldorf 21
Federweisser, young white wine 71
Fennel salad with herbs 30
Filled Pancake Strips 31
Fish
    Creamy sauce for Matjes 46
    Haddock fillets in creamy mustard sauce baked with vegetable julienne 40
    Herring fillets 46
    Marinated Salmon à la Ingeborg 44
    Matjes (young herring fillets) with new potatoes in a creamy sauce 46
    Mecklenburg fish ragout 86
    Sole with carrot cream on risotto and kohlrabi 67
Fish ragout Mecklenburg 86
Flat parsley 98
Formula 1 car racing 78
Fruit
    Rhubarb-vanilla cream 45
    Rote Grütze with vanilla ice cream or yogurt cream 17
    Rumtopf (fruit in Rum) 46

G

Garlic 98
Garlic Leaf/wild garlic (Baerlauch) 98
Gelatin 97
German Cheese Cake with raisins 24
German History 2
German pancakes 81
German Wine Institute 100
Gewürztraminer 87

Glatte Petersilie 98
Glühwein 95
Goulash soup 52
Grapes 100
Gratin of potatoes 75
Grauburgunder (Gray Burgundy or Pinot Grigio) 100

H

Haddock fillets in creamy mustard sauce baked with vegetable julienne 40
Hanse 4, 84
Hanseatic League 4, 84
Hare, sweet and sour 96
Hasenpfeffer 96
Hefebier 99
Herbed soup 86
Herbs and spices 98
    Artemisia 98
    Arugula 98
    Baerlauch 98
    Basil 98
    Basilikum 98
    Beifuss 98
    Brunnenkresse 98
    Chervil 98
    Chives 98
    Curly parsley 98
    Dill 98
    Estragon 98
    Flat parsley 98
    Garlic 98
    Garlic Leaf or wild garlic 98
    Glatte Petersilie 98
    Kerbel 98
    Knoblauch 98
    Koriander 98
    Liebstoeckel 98
    Love parsley 98
    Maggi 98
    Majoran 98
    Marjoram 98
    Mint 98
    Minze 98
    Mugwort 98
    Oregano 98
    Oreganum 98
    Parsley, curlz 98
    Parsley flat 98
    Petersilie 98
    Rosemary 98

Rosmarin 98
Rukola 98
Sage 98
Salbei 98
Sauerampfer 98
Schnittlauch 98
Sorrel 98
Tarragon 98
Thyme 98
Thymian 98
Watercress 98

Herring fillets 46

Herring Salad 18

Himmel und Erde (Heaven and Earth) with chicken liver or fried black pudding 54

History 3
A Little German History 2
Bohemia 3
Hanse", the Hanseatic League 4
Prussia 3

Hollandaise sauce 45

Horseradish cream dressing 86

I

Iceberg lettuce with almond lemon dressing 32

Idstein 90

Internet Resources
Food Facts 114
Locations 113

Iron Curtain 84

Italian dressing 58

J

January in Xanten 15

Julienne of leek and carrot 80

July in Frankfurt am Main 57

June in Köln (Cologne) 51

K

Kabinett 100
Karneval 21
Kerbel 98
Kirschmichel (Cherry Crumble) 60
Knoblauch 98
Kö 21
Koblenz 64
Kohlrabi 67

Kohlrouladen (pigs in a blanket) with potatoes, carrots, and gravy 52
Kölner Dom (Cologne Cathedral) 50
Kölsch 99
Kölsch beer 53
Königsallee 21
Koriander 98
Krause Petersilie 98

L

Lactose 101
Lactose and Gluten free sauce 101
Lactose-free 17
Lager 99
Lambs' lettuce (Feldsalat) with mustard dressing and bacon crumbles 17
Landwein 100
Langenberg 37
Leek 97
Leek Quiche 22
Leftover dish
Tafelspitz salad 34
Leftover Special 39
Calf tongue salad with mushrooms 39
Lemon dressing with walnuts or pumpkin seeds 52
Lemon tarragon dressing 81
Lent 21
Liebstoeckel 98
Light colored beers
Berliner Weisse 99
Hefebier 99
Helles Bier 99
Lager beers 99
Lime vinaigrette 92
Loin of deer with Brussels sprouts and Semmelknödel (bread dumplings) 92
Lorraine 64
Lovage 98
Lovage, also known as love parsley (Liebstoeckel): 98
Love parsley 98
Lower Saxony 42

M

Maggi 98
Maggi Würze, Maggi seasoning 98

Index

Majoran 98
Mandarin oranges 66
Manderscheid Castle 78
March in Berlin 29
Mardi Gras 21
Marinated Salmon à la Ingeborg 44
Marjoram 98
Marrow Dumplings 59
Mashed potatoes with Portobello mushrooms 73
Matjes (young herring fillets) with new potatoes in a creamy sauce 46
May in Osnabrück 43
Meatloaves 68
Mecklenburg fish ragout 86
Mecklenburg-Vorpommern 84
Meerrettichlende (or Tafelspitz), beef loin with horseradish and chives cream 32
Meissen 90
Merlot 81
Mini meatloaves in mushroom sauce 68
Mint 98
Minze 98
Mixed greens with cream of chives 73
Mock turtle soup (my family version) 22
Morcheln 101
Morels 101
Mosel 64
Moselle 64
Mosel-Saar-Ruwer region 64
Mousse of Chocolate 74
Mousse of peaches 67
Mugwort 98
Mulled red wine 95
Mushroom cream sou 72
Mushroom ragout with Pfannekuchen (German pancakes) 80
Mushrooms
    Austernpilze 101
    Boletos 101
    Champignons 101
    Chanterelles 101
    Criminis 101
    Morcheln 101
    Morels 101
    Oyster mushrooms 101
    Pfifferlinge 101
    Portobellos 101
    Steinpilze 101
    Wiesenchampignon 101
Mushroom salad with garlic lemon vinaigrette 53
Mushroom sauce 59
Mushroom sauce for meatloaves 68
Mushroom Schnitzel with green beans in creamy mushroom sauce 59
Mushrooms in Europe 101
Mustard dressing 17, 60

N

Neuss 90
New Year's Herring Salad 18
Niederrhein region 14
November on the Baltic Sea 85
Nürburgring 78

O

Obergärig 99
October in the Eifel Mountains 79
Oktoberfest beer 99
Onion pie 72
Onions and yogurt dressing 16
Orange and horseradish cream dressing 86
Orange-caper dressing 30
Oregano 98
Oreganum 98
Orvieto 53
Osnabrück 42
Osnabrücker Land 42
Oyster mushrooms 101

P

Pancake strips for soups 30
Parsley Dumplings 59
Parsley flat 98
Pasta salad with white crab meat 80
Peaches to the Rumtopf 57
Peach Mousse 67
Pears sautéed in red Burgundy wine 74
Pears to the Rumtopf 79
Petersilie 98

Pfalz (Palatine) wines   100
Pfannekuchen (German pancakes)   81
Pfannekuchenstreifen (pancake strips)   30
Pfifferlinge   101
Pflaumenkuchen (Plumcake)   81
Pheasant with wine sauerkraut and Portobello mashed potatoes   72
Pigs in a blanket   52
Pilsner   81, 99
Pilsner or another light beer   17
Pinot Grigio   39, 53
Pinot Noir   23, 93
Plums to the Rumtopf   71
Pork tenderloin in beer sauce with apples and cranberries, dried fruit compote or creamed savoy cabbage   82
Portobello mashed potatoes   73
Portobellos   101
Potatoes   97
Potato gratin   75
Potato pancakes   95
Potato salad Biedermeier   87
Potato soup with leek julienne   38
Puff pastry   31, 39
Pumpkin seeds   52
Pumpkin soup with julienned leek and carrot   80

Q

Qualitätswein   100
Quark   97
Quiche Sauerkraut   61

R

Rabbit in white wine sauce, paired with Karin's potato gratin   74
Ragout from calf tongue with a side dish of cauliflower baked in puff pastry   38
Red Burgundy   93, 100
Red cabbage   23
Red cabbage and Thuringian dumplings   23
Red onion vinaigrette   60
Red wine   100
Red Wine Trail   70
Red Zinfandel   23, 60, 73

References   113
Reibekuchen (potato pancakes)   95
Reinheitsgebot   99
Reisflammeri   32
Religious wars   42
Remagen   70
Rhine river   50
Rhubarb-vanilla cream   45
Rice
    Risotto   67
Riesling   32, 67
Risotto   67
Romaine lettuce with creamy mustard dressing and walnuts   39
Romaine lettuce with lemon tarragon dressing   81
Rosemary   98
Rose wine   100
Rosmarin   98
Rote Grütze with vanilla ice cream or yogurt cream   17
Roter Spätburgunder (Red Burgundy) from Germany   60
Rotweinstrasse   70
Rotweinwanderweg   70
Rouladen (stuffed beef) with a stew of carrots and potatoes "Durcheinander"   16
Ruhrgebiet   21
Rukola   98
Rumtopf
    Apples to the Rumtopf   85
    Apricots to the Rumtopf   65
    Cherries to the Rumtopf   51
    Enjoy your Rumtopf - with a scoop of vanilla ice cream or vanilla puddin   91
    Peaches to the Rumtopf   57
    Pears to the Rumtopf   79
    Plums to the Rumtopf   71
Rumtopf (fruit in Rum)   46

S

Saar-Mosel-Ruwer   78
Sage   98
Salad
    Iceberg lettuce with almond lemon dressing   32
    Pfannekuchenstreifen as garnish for salad or soup   30
    Spinach salad iwith mustard dressing   60
    Tafelspitz salad   34

Index

Tomato salad with red onion vinaigrette and Spinach salad with mustard dressing   60
Salbei   98
Salmon, marinated   44
Sauce
   Apple Horseradish Sauce (Apfelkren)   33
   Carrot cream   67
   Chives cream   33
   Creamy sauce for Matjes   46
   Hollandaise sauce   45
   Mushroom sauce   59
   Mushroom sauce for meatloaves   68
   Vanilla sauce from scratch   94
   White wine sauce for rabbit   74
Sauerampfer   98
Sauerbraten with Red Cabbage, Thuringian dumplings and applesauce with cranberries   22
Sauerkraut quiche   61
Sauvignon Blanc   87
Savoy Cabbage creamed   82
Schloss Burg   36
Schwarzbrot (dark whole rye bread)   26
Schwerin   84
Sekt   100
Semmelknödel (bread dumplings)   93
Semolina dumplings   66
September in the Ahr Valley   71
Sherry wine   92
Shiraz   73
Side dish
   Applesauce with cranberries   24
   Brussels sprouts   93
   Carrot and potato dish (Durcheinander)   17
   Cauliflower baked in puff pastry   39
   Dried fruit compote   82
   Kohlrabi   67
   Mashed potatoes with Portobello mushrooms   73
   Portobello mashed potatoes   73
   Potato gratin   75
   Red Cabbage   23
   Risotto   67
   Savoy Cabbage creamed   82
   Semmelknödel (bread dumplings)   93
   Thuringian Dumplings   23
   Wine sauerkraut with grapes   73
Side salad
   Arugula salad with vinaigrette, cranberries and walnut   93
   Biedermeier potato salad   87
   Carrot salad with sweet and sour dressing   45
   Cucumber salad in dill dressing   67
   Iceberg lettuce with almond lemon dressing   32
   Lambs' lettuce (Feldsalat)   17
   Mixed greens with cream of chives   73
   Mushroom salad with garlic lemon vinaigrette   53
   Romaine lettuce with creamy mustard dressing and walnuts   39
   Romaine lettuce with lemon tarragon dressing   81
   Tomato salad with red onion vinaigrette   60
Sole with carrot cream on risotto and kohlrabi   67
Sorrel (Sauerampfer)   98
Soup   9, 16
   Bouillon, chicken   66
   Chicken bouillon with semolina dumpling   66
   Clear asparagus soup with asparagus pieces   44
   Clear beef bouillon with pancake strips   30
   Clear tomato soup   16
   Creamed potato soup with leek julienne   38
   Creamed Tomato soup with sherry wine   92
   Goulash soup   52
   Herbed soup   86
   Mock turtle soup   22
   Mushroom cream soup   72
   Pancake strips for soups   30
   Pfannekuchenstreifen as garnish for soup or salad   30
   Potato soup with leek julienne   38
   Pumpkin soup with julienned leek and carrot   80
   Vegetable soup with egg dumplings   58
Soups and sauces   97
Sour cream dressing   66
Spätburgunder   93
Spätburgunder Weissherbst (Rose Burgundy)   100
Spätlese   100
Special dish
   Beef loin with apples, plums, and potatoes   88
   Erbsensuppe (split pea soup)   25
   Haddock fillets in creamy mustard sauce baked with vegetable julienne   40
   Hasenpfeffer   96
   Himmel und Erde (Heaven and Earth) with chicken liver or fried black pudding   54
   Matjes (young herring fillets) with new potatoes in a creamy sauce   46
   Meerrettichlende (or Tafelspitz), beef loin with horseradish and chives cream   32
   Mini meatloaves in mushroom sauce   68
   New Year's Herring Salad   18
   Pork tenderloin in beer sauce with apples and cranberries, dried fruit compote or creamed savoy cabbage   82
   Rabbit in white wine sauce, paired with Karin's potato gratin   74
   Reibekuchen (potato pancakes)   95

Sauerkraut quiche 61
Spekulatius cookies 94
Spinach salad iwith mustard dressing 60
Steinpilze 101
St. James pilgrimage way 78
St. Nikolaus 90
Substitute butter 101
Substitute sugar and wine 101
Suppengemüse 21
Sweet and sour dressing 45
Sweet rice in red wine with whipped cream 32

T

Table wine 100
Tafelspitz 32
Tafelspitz salad 34
Tafelwein 100
Tarragon (Estragon) 98
The Menus of the Month 9
The Wall 84
Thuringian dumplings 23
Thyme 98
Thymian 98
To brown meat without additional fat 101
Tomato salad with red onion vinaigrette and Spinach salad with mustard dressing 60
Treves 65
Trier 64
Trockenbeerenauslese 100

U

Untergärig 99

V

Vanilla sauce from scratch 94
Vegetable
    Brussels sprouts 93
    Kohlrabi 67
Vegetables and their Seasons 97
Vegetable soup with egg dumplings 58
Venison 92
Venues 9
    April in the Bergische Land 37
    August on the Mosel River 65
    December at the Christmas Markets 91
    February in Düsseldorf 21
    January in Xanten 15
    July in Frankfurt am Main 57
    June in Köln (Cologne) 51
    March in Berlin 29
    May in Osnabrück 43
    November on the Baltic Sea 85
    October in the Eifel Mountains 79
    September in the Ahr Valley 71
Vinaigrette with cranberries and walnuts 93

W

Warnow 84
Watercress 98
Weisser Burgunder (White Burgundy, also a Chardonnay grape) 100
Weizenbier 99
Westphalian Peace 42
White asparagus 44
White Burgundy 45
White wine 100
White wine sauce for rabbit 74
Wiesenchampignon 101
Wine
    Auslese 100
    Austrian Wines 100
    Beerenauslese 100
    Cabernet Sauvignon 23
    Chardonnay 39
    Eiswein 100
    Gewürztraminer 87, 100
    Glühwein 95
    Grapes 100
    Grauburgunder (Gray Burgundy or Pinot Grigio) 100
    Landwein 100
    Merlot 81
    Mulled red wine 95
    Orvieto 53
    Pinot Grigio 39, 53
    Pinot Noir 23, 93
    Qualitätswein 100
    Red Burgundy 93, 100
    Red Zinfandel 23, 60, 73
    Riesling 67, 100
    Riesling white wine 32
    Rose wine 100
    Roter Spätburgunder (Red Burgundy) from Germany 60
    Sauvignon Blanc 87
    Sekt 100
    Shiraz 73
    Silvaner 100

Spätburgunder 93
Spätburgunder (Red Burgundy) 100
Spätburgunder Weissherbst (Rose Burgundy) 100
Spätlese 100
Table wine 100
Tafelwein 100
Trockenbeerenauslese 100
Weisser Burgunder (White Burgundy, also a Chardonnay grape) 100
White Burgundy 45
Wine Cream 87
Wine-growing areas in Germany 100
Wine sauerkraut with grapes 73
Wuppertal 37

X
Xanten, Niederrhein 13

Y
Yogurt cake 24

Z
Zwetschgen 81
Zwiebelkuchen 72

References

Although a great number of these recipes have been an important part of my growing up in a big family, I didn't have all of them written down when I started this project.

As a result, I dug through my mother's recipes, contacted friends and family members, and went through cook books I bought in Germany. Everybody who inherits old family recipes knows those "a little bit of this and a little bit of that, then stir frequently and don't forget not to lift the cover of the pot!" kind of handed-down recipes, so what I needed to do was to look up today's recipes and change them so that they matched the taste and tradition of the ones I had inherited.

I have an extensive collection of German and European cookbooks, and it would be too much to list all of them. All of them have been converted to American standards and available food.

Also, if you would like to do some research about the locations, here are some websites you can use for your own "digging."

Have fun!

Locations:
Unfortunately, most of German cities' websites don't have an English site available. Where I found one, though, I have marked it behind the URL of the website.

To learn more about facts world wide, here is is one of the great websites where you can find facts about almost any country around the globe:

The CIA (American Central Intelligence Agency):
http://www.cia.gov/cia/publications/factbook/
http://www.yourchildlearns.com/europe_map.htm

And now here's the rest of my list:

The World Tourism Organization
http://www.world-tourism.org/
http://www.towd.com/ (World Directory of Tourist Offices)

United States of America
http://factfinder.census.gov/jsp/saff/SAFFInfo.jsp?_pageId=gt1_site_map
http://usinfo.state.gov/usa/infousa/facts/facts.htm

Europe and the European Union
http://europa.eu.int/index_en.htm

Germany (in general)
http://www.germanculture.com.ua/library/facts/bl_germany.htm
http://www.baedeker.com/index.php
http://www.germany-tourism.de/index.html

Germany's Scenic Routes
http://www.germany-tourism.de/e/scenic_routes.html (English)

History of Germany and Europe
http://www.roadstoruins.com/history1.html (English)

The German Cities and Regions:
Xanten and the Lower Rhine Land
http://www.niederrhein-tourismus.de/2005/english/welcome.php (english)
http://www.germany-tourism.de/e/city_xanten.html (english)
Image of Roter Heringssalat source: http://www.lecker.de

Düsseldorf, Capital of North Rhine Westphalia)
http://www.duesseldorf.de/de/
Photo of Schwarzbrot: Photo: www.drinnen-und-draussen.de

The Ruhrgebiet
http://www.historisches-centrum.de/ruhrgebiet/

Berlin in Mark Brandenburg
http://www.berlin.de/english/index.html (English)
http://www.brandenburg.de/cms/detail.php?template=site_detail&id=11345&_siteid=75 (English)
Image Tafelspitz Salad: http://mellonblog.de

Langenberg (City of Velbert) in Rhine Land
http://www.velbert.de/stadtinfo/stadtrundgang/langenberg.asp
http://www.bergisches-land.de/

Osnabrück in Lower Saxony (all English)
http://www.osnabrueck.de/
Region: http://www.niedersachsen-tourism.de/en/regionen-staedte/regionen/osnabruecker_land/index.php

References

Cologne in Rhine Land
http://www.germany-tourism.de/e/dest_cities_koeln_e.html (English)
http://www.stadt-koeln.de/en/koelntourismus/index.html (English)

Recipe for blood pudding:
http://www.sausagelinks.co.uk/blackpudding.htm#cookingblackpudding
Image source: http://horrmann.luxus.welt.de

Frankfurt am Main (on Main river in Hessia)
http://www.frankfurt.de/sis/English.html (English)

Cochem on the Mosel river and the Mosel-Saar-Ruwer wine area
http://www.mosel-reisefuehrer.de/cochem.htm
http://www.germanwine.de/english/d_reg/r_mos.htm

Ahrweiler and the Ahr river valley, and its wine regions in the Eifel area
http://www.bad-neuenahr-ahrweiler-online.de/
http://www.alt-ahrweiler.de/123.htm

Eifel
http://www.eifel-online.de/
Image rurstausee: http://www.urlaub-in-rheinland-pfalz.de

Warnemünde on the Baltic Sea in Mecklenburg Vorpommern
http://www.auf-nach-mv.de/home2.html? (English)
http://www.all-in-all.com/index.htm (English)

The Hanse Trade Association
http://www.hanse.org/index.php?lg=en (English)

Christmas Markets
http://www.germany-christmas-market.org.uk/index1.htm (English)
http://en.wikipedia.org/wiki/St._Nikolaus (English)
Image of Glühwein source: www.duden.de
Image Reibekuchen source: www.chefkoch.de

General Information
http://www.encyclopedia.com/
http://encarta.msn.com/

Food facts:
The Cook's Thesaurus (a wonderful website with more information than you could wish for)
http://www.foodsubs.com/

All about German beer
http://www.fosters.com.au/beer/history/history_of_beer.asp (English)

All about wine (keywords germany wine)
History of Wine: http://www.chiff.com/wine/history.htm (English)
All about German wines: http://www.germanwine.de/english/
http://www.germanwineestates.com/ (English)
http://www.germanwinesociety.org/regions.html

Vegetable harvest schedule, when is which vegetable farm fresh available?
http://www.homestead-farm.net/HarvestSch.html

Where to buy some specialties if you can't make them:

Fondor (Maggi)
http://www.germandeli.com/index.html

Gelatin:
http://www.kraftfoods.com/knox/knox_gelatine.html

Schwarzbrot (Whole Rye Bread):
http://www.schwarzbrot.com/

Mustard:
German Food, a general store, where I found items like the original Dusseldorf mustard or also Lowensenf:
http://www.deutscheshaus.cc/html/german_food.html (English)

Quark:
I also found Quark in a "Deutsches Haus" and the clerk told me that all "Deutsche Haus" shops carry this cheese.
http://www.deutscheshaus.cc/html/german_food.html
Another source is the Appel Farms in California
http://www.appel-farms.com/pages/the_dairy.html
http://www.germandeli.com/040817010014.html

Thank You

Special thanks to my husband for his courage and patience: he was the one who had to eat what I cooked; my family and friends in America for their support, advice, and active help.

To Rhoda and Tom Lewin, the editors of the first edition: their contribution and encouragement went far beyond mere editing.

Editing photography is a strain on the eyes, so here are my heartfelt thanks to my fellow photographer, Yolanda vom Hagen, for her generous help in editing the photography of this book.

To all my friends and family in Germany: thank you for all the recipes and contributions of cultural background, family traditions, historic facts and stories about your German heritage.

I probably should thank all the authors on the Internet who contributed to this book without knowing. I spent endless hours searching the web for history, maps, stories and information about German history, German customs, German cities and their past and present. And I hope I gave the appropriate credit to all of them in the "Resources" section of this book.

Ute Buehler

www.ingramcontent.com/pod-product-compliance
Lightning Source LLC
Chambersburg PA
CBHW041121300426
44112CB00003B/54